SPECIAL AMERICAN LEGION EDITION   COPY #S 2014-0050

1ST EDITION
1ST PRINTING
SOFT COVER

MW01195546

THANKS FOR HELPING OUR
NEEDY VETERANS AND THEIR FAMILIES!

4/14/2014

INSIDE THE WORLD OF MIRRORS

The Story of a Shadow Warrior

J. Max Taylor

authorHOUSE®

AuthorHouse™
1663 Liberty Drive
Bloomington, IN 47403
www.authorhouse.com
Phone: 1-800-839-8640

© 2013 J. Max Taylor. All rights reserved.

No part of this book may be reproduced, stored in a retrieval system, or transmitted by any means without the written permission of the author.

Published by AuthorHouse 3/29/2013

ISBN: 978-1-4817-1858-5 (sc)
ISBN: 978-1-4817-1859-2 (hc)
ISBN: 978-1-4817-1868-4 (e)

Library of Congress Control Number: 2013903138

Any people depicted in stock imagery provided by Thinkstock are models, and such images are being used for illustrative purposes only. Certain stock imagery © Thinkstock.

This book is printed on acid-free paper.

Because of the dynamic nature of the Internet, any web addresses or links contained in this book may have changed since publication and may no longer be valid. The views expressed in this work are solely those of the author and do not necessarily reflect the views of the publisher, and the publisher hereby disclaims any responsibility for them.

Table of Contents

<u>Dedication</u>

This book is about the unseen Shadow War that occurred between 1968 and 1976. It was written to honor those who served our country and didn't come back. They may have been ignored or denied by the "Powers That Be", but they will live in my heart and my nightmares as long as I live. A portion of the proceeds of this book will go to help homeless veterans.

Two special people in my life made it possible for me to write this book. Without their help, inspiration, and support this book would have never happened.

The first and most important is my wonderful supportive wife Dorothy. She loved and helped me move forward for over 35 years. Without her love and healing touch these words could never have been written.

The second is Chris Powers, a disabled veteran, who stood by me during the period from 2001 to the present. His help and understanding helped carry me through the many trips I took into my nightmare's horrors that dominated my life during this time.

__Introduction__

There is a special world deep inside of the U.S. Intelligence community that has been referred to as the **"World of Mirrors"**. It never officially existed, but was hiding behind so many different reflections that it could never be found. This book will take you on a short journey and go __"Inside the World of Mirrors"__

This is the story of one man's experience in Special Intelligence Operations (SIO) from 1968-1976 in the War being fought against the Communist and Terrorist enemies of our country.

The stories of the missions in this book have no written record to verify them. In addition, no agency of the United States Government will admit to any knowledge of any of these activities or operations.

You may choose to consider that everything in this book is a total work of fiction, or you could take a hard look at the way the hottest "Cold War" was actually fought.

Most people have heard the term "Black Operations" used to describe highly classified missions. Only a very few people know that there is a classification above BlackOps.

Within the tiny community of people that lived, suffered, and died __"Inside the World of Mirrors"__ it was referred as the "Shadow War". Every mission was verbally authorized. Any information you received was limited to what the decision makers deemed was a necessary minimum.

SIO personnel were seldom told the whole truth but instead were given just enough information to keep them in trouble. The "Powers that Be" referred to it as "Need to Know."

I have many times wondered that if the man doing the work does not need to know the facts, then who does need to know?

This is a story of how things really worked. The times displayed in this book are shown in the standard government/military 24 hour mode.

The names have been changed to protect the privacy of any of the few people that still happen to be alive. The missions set forth herein are as real as the stories in your morning newspaper.

Chapter 1
The Chinese Shooting Gallery

After many months of training in intelligence and Special Intelligence Operations (SIO) techniques, I had been sent to Seoul Korea as an "Intelligence Editor" at 8th Army. I was there for about 5 months when the CIA Chief of Station (COS) at the U.S. Embassy called me. I agreed to meet him at the embassy at 1400. I had met David Rhinehart before, so when I got to the embassy, they took me upstairs to his office. We sat down at a conference table, and drank coffee while the rest of his staff came in.

When his staff was finally seated at the table, it was obvious that something big was going on. The entire table had been covered with maps and imagery of an area about 5 kilometers inside of North Vietnam. They wanted to put together a special mission, and had a small 48 hour window to plan and execute a mission team into the area.

Somewhere in the chain of intelligence, it had determined that a high ranking Chinese officer and, probably, one or two of his staff were going to be inspecting a series of sites which the North Vietnamese Army (NVA) regulars were using for special training activities.

The next TET (Vietnam's New Year celebration) offensive was about 10 weeks out, and intelligence reports indicated that this would be a very active TET because of the special training and advanced equipment that was being supplied to the NVA by the Peoples Republic of China (PRC).

David had been instructed to send in a sniper team to take out the Chinese officers. It was thought that if the Chinese officers were killed while in North Vietnam, that the repercussions would cause difficulties in the North Vietnamese government's relations with China. The equipment being supplied represented by the largest commitment of materials that the PRC had ever provided.

David's usual operation teams were already out in the field on other missions. He said it wasn't possible to get them back into the base, brief them, and send them back out in time.

While I had been trained to a high level, this would be the first time that I would actually go into the field as a sniper. This made me a little nervous, but also charged me up. I would finally have an opportunity perform the mission I had been trained to do.

The mission specifications called for a chopper insertion about 15 kilometers from the training area. I would have two Special Forces personnel and two Montenyards (indigenous personnel sometimes referred to as Yards) that were familiar with the area. They had run missions into the general area before, but only for intelligence gathering. This would be the first active attack mission to be run in this area of North Vietnam.

David told me that he had a C-130 waiting at Kimpo Air Base. It was about a 40 minute drive to get there, and they were fueled and ready to take off immediately. He had my field kit, which I always had stored with Security at the Embassy. It included my jungle uniform, sniper rifle and 2 scopes, my silenced pistol, and other equipment. It was ready for me to take with me when I got on the plane.

I expressed my concern that the 15 kilometer infiltration would be almost impossible to accomplish in the time frame we would have available. In areas where the enemy forces were present in large numbers, it was difficult to move more than 4 or 5 kilometers maximum in a night. If you moved faster than that, you were probably going to be seen, heard, or found. If you were noticed prior to starting your attack, then it was highly probable that you would not be coming back.

We looked for, and found an insertion point much closer to the NVA training area. It was only about 5 kilometers from the target area.

The only problem was that the LZ was too small for the helicopter to land in. We would have to go down by rope. This was actually a good thing. The small size of the LZ was actually an advantage, as it probably would not have trail watchers or an ambush set up in the area.

When no enemy fire took place during an insertion or an extraction by helicopter, it was called a "Cold LZ (Landing Zone)". If there were any enemy troops present, then it was called a "Hot LZ".

The site we chose was usable for an insertion, but not practical for an extraction. The closest set of extraction points were between 5 and 8 kilometers further away from the training area.

David agreed to my proposed rope insertion and the alternate extraction points. Ten minutes later I was in a car on the way to Kimpo Air Force Base. An hour later I boarded the C-130 and we took off. The layout of the C-130 included a sleeping area for the backup crew to use on long flights. This would only be a short flight, so I went to the crew quarters, put on headphones to block out the noise, and lay down to sleep. I was going to need all the sleep and rest I could get.

I woke up when we landed at Nakhon Phanom. This was a special operations base for Central Intelligence Agency (CIA) activities and was located in the northern portion of Cambodia. My first impression was quickly and permanently imprinted in my brain. It had a smell like nothing else I had ever been exposed to.

A jeep took me to the Tactical Operations Center (TOC) and I met the mission control officer (MCO), the Forward Air Controller (FAC) that would be supporting us, and the rest of the mission team. The team included 2 green berets and 2 Montenyards. We spent about 3 hours discussing the mission.

We then ate a high protein meal, and prepped all our equipment. My primary weapon was the AK-47 developed by Automat Kalashnikov in the Soviet Union. The team was surprised when I pulled out my LC-1A sniper rifle, checked the scopes, and loaded it up in a case I slung over my shoulder. They were surprised because it was such a strange looking weapon.

It had 23" of barrel beyond the stock, and was supported by a bi-pod providing a stable firing position. In addition it was a single shot weapon with a model 1887 brass nitrogen filled scope and a sighting scope mounted beside the targeting scope. The team looked at me as if I were a little crazy. I would be carrying the LC-1A in a case over my shoulder, and an AK-47 in hand to be ready if we got into a fire fight. In addition, I always carried a 22 berretta with a silencer just in case I needed to wage a quiet war.

We were soon ready and headed for the helicopter that was taking us in. We loaded up, and were airborne in less than 15 minutes. The flight took about 2 hours. When we were about 30 minutes from our insertion point, we started putting on all our gear, and getting the repelling ropes attached and ready for use.

At 5 minutes out we were standing on the skids of the chopper, hands on the ropes, and ready for the signal to go. The helicopter suddenly slowed down and came to a hover over a small opening in the jungle canopy. They gave us the go signal and down we went. This was the point where the adrenaline really started to pump. If any of the enemy were on the ground around the insertion point, we would be in big trouble.

It took about 20 seconds for everyone to reach the ground. We immediately ran to the edge of the clearing into the bush and hit the ground. In the time that it took for us to get there the chopper was already gone. It's was a strange feeling to know that the only backup and your ride home had just left. We were on our own now. Fortunately, the LZ was cold as we had hoped it would be.

After about 15 minutes, we moved out. In another 30 minutes it was completely dark. The trip to the site was right out of the training manual as I had been taught in Panama.

At no time did we come close to walking on a trail. We had a point man out in front of us about 20 meters. Behind him walking slack was a Green Beret with a Machine Gun. The rest of us followed ten meters behind him. We walked about 3 meters apart so that one grenade would not get us all. The last man in our group was walking backward about half the time making sure we were not being followed.

We would move about 10 – 15 meters, stop and listen for a minute or two, then move again. This continued until 2100 hours, when we back tracked and looped around into some deep bush to take a short break and make sure we were not being followed.

Moving through the bush and making no noise is extremely

stressful and tiring. Silence was the only chance we had when you were up against at least 1000 NVA within a 2 square mile area. We needed to take a break from time to time or we would get sloppy and something bad would happen. At 2115 we moved out again using the same movement procedure.

About 0300 we found the trail that we were looking for. It took about 30 minutes to find a well-concealed hide with a good shooting position. We back tracked and looped around to the site while checking for anyone that might be following us. Once we were sure that we weren't being followed, we moved about fifty meters into our hide.

The site was perfect for me. I had a clear line of sight, about 200 meters, down a valley with a trail beside a creek. I had my LC-1A rifle and model 1887 scope assembled.

We put out the Montenyards about 20 meters away for extra security. The two green berets were still with me, one about 5 meters away, and the other within a couple of feet of me. Now the hard part began. Waiting for the NVA with Chinese officers to come walking along a trail between two of the largest training sites was both boring and exciting.

About 0700, a group of approximately 30 NVA came down the trail, but they didn't have any Chinese officers with them. At 0850, another large group passed. Just like the first group, they had no Chinese officers with them.

At 1115, another group came down the trail. It was very different from the other two groups. It only had 10 or 12 members walking single file. In the middle of the column were two brown uniforms with shoulder tabs. The Chinese officers had finally appeared.

I signaled the team that I was about to take the primary targets under fire. No one else would shoot until I had fired two shots or had taken more than 10 seconds to take the second shot, then everyone would hit the formation with everything we had.

It was amazing how aware of every sensation I was. I could feel the air move the hairs on the back of my hands and arms. The adrenalin high was full blown. If it was raining, I think I could have walked between the drops of rain and never got wet. I took aim at the center of the chest of the leading Chinese officer.

I pulled back on the trigger to the arming point, and then began to add more pressure. As was usual, my concentration was on my sight picture and the delicate pull on the trigger. It almost always surprised me when the weapon fired. I hit center mass on the target. I reloaded and aimed at the second Chinese officer. For some reason, they had not got down on the ground, but were still standing up in confusion. I took out the second Chinese officer the same way, and the rest of the group began to fire into the NVA.

After about 30 seconds, I yelled out the word "Rebound". It was a signal for the team to back away from the ambush. The Montenyards took off first and ran till they were about 20 meters behind the rest of us. They then started firing at the remainder of the column and the rest of us ran uphill till we were past the Montenyards. We hit the ground, started firing at what little was left of the column, and the Montenyards ran back to where we were.

We all then took off running further up the hillside into the deep brush. We had to clear the immediate area as quickly as possible. But we couldn't run on the trails, because that is where the enemy would be coming from.

After about 15 minutes, I had us slow down and go into quiet movement mode. We would move for about 30 seconds, then stop and listen. If we heard or saw nothing, we would repeat the process. As we moved, we kept moving away from the trail and into the deeper brush.

During one period when we were stopped and listening we heard the sound of metal clinking. When you run in the jungle, unless you had taken special preparations on your gear, your equipment would make metallic noises. This could be solved by taking precautions such as carefully taping all loose metal that you were wearing, never having your canteen half full, and never talking. All communications were done by hand signals.

We immediately went prone on the ground and crawled behind the nearest tree or bush. This group didn't see us, and they kept running back up the trail toward the initial attack area. As soon as they passed and were out of sight, we got up and started moving again.

This went on for about 2 more hours without being seen. We found a good hide and crawled inside the brush and brambles and set up in a circle with our feet in the center. Everyone had their weapon pointed out and ready to fire.

We put out three claymore mines. Two were aimed at potential attack areas, and one was setup to clear an emergency escape path through the brush behind us.

I watched several other groups go by without seeing us. It was starting to get dark again, so we retrieved our claymore mines, and started out again using our quiet movement mode of travel.

Several times we saw patrols working areas ahead of us. We would wait until the patrol had passed through the area, then we would go to where they had just been. It seemed odd when I was first told about this in training back in Panama, but it proved to be true. The NVA just doesn't search for someone where they had just looked five minutes ago.

About 1930 we found another good hide, and went into full defensive mode. We put out 3 claymores on the most likely approaches to our position. Then we backed up into our circle formation to try to get some rest.

Two people would be on watch all the time. Each watch lasted for an hour. At the end of that time, the next two people would take the watch. When you were not on watch, you ate, cleaned your weapon, and tried to get some rest.

We had caused quite a stir with the NVA. They were beginning to patrol not just the trail, but the areas on each side of the trail. Each patrol would have 25 to 30 NVA in it. If we were to get into a fire fight, our only hope was that the claymore mines would even up the odds a little.

The NVA were obviously very upset at losing the two Chinese officers. We saw 4 patrols pass us in less than 2 hours. I pulled in close to the senior Green Beret and discussed the high number of NVA patrols. I also told him that I would expect that a number of ambushes would be set out by night time. This would make the evenings movement even more dangerous.

We went over the maps, and decided to follow the next patrol going west. I had been told that the NVA patrols would often stop and talk to any NVA ambushes that they were passing while on patrol.

This would tell us where to take a wide detour and still help us keep covert.

About 2300 a NVA patrol came by heading west. We slipped out of our hide and followed them. One of the Montenyards was walking point about 20 meters ahead of the rest of our team. The other Montenyard was walking in the trail position to watch our back track for signs of movement.

The NVA patrol was somewhat casual as they moved down the trail. We had been following them for about 30 minutes, when the point man of the patrol, turned around and said something to the next man in line. That man turned and talked to the man behind him, and so it continued until everyone in the patrol had received the message from the point man. Things immediately changed. The patrol stepped off the trail about 5 meters to the right side, and then began walking parallel to the trail.

It took a moment or two to realize that what I was seeing was a bobby-trap area along the trail. It was obvious that to walk on the trail along this area was not a good idea. This was only one of the reasons that we always walked a considerable distance away from the trails and in dense brush.

After about 100 meters the point man turned around and signaled toward the trail. The patrol followed him back onto the path, and continued on.

About 500 meters further on, we saw the point man shoulder his weapon, and walk off the trail to the left side and go up hill with the patrol following him. Within a few moments, we saw another soldier stand up and wave to the point man.

We had just discovered an ambush position. The patrol personnel and the ambush position personnel sat down to talk and eat. It was all so casual that it made the hair stand up on the back of my neck.

The ambush was well positioned, and we probably would not have seen them. They were dug in under and behind bushes. We backed up about 200 meters, and I waved everyone to come to me. I explained what we had seen, and we decided to go over the top of the hill to the left behind the ambush, and then continue on. We would stay as far away from trails as was possible. We continued on till about 0400, when we found another good site to lay up in during the day. We had seen two other patrols, but no more evidence of ambush positions. Our pace of advance had slowed down considerably because of the concern about running into more booby-trapped areas.

We set out some claymores, and backed into our hide for the day. I was quietly woken up about 0730 by one of the Montenyards. I had only been off watch for about 30 minutes, so I knew that something was going on.

I crawled over to the side of our hide, and watched in amazement as a full NVA engineering team was digging along the side of a trail about 60 meters below our location. Then I realized that they were putting out another bobby-trapped position. The part that worried me most was that they had people working and extending the position about 30 meters on either side of the trail. This gave me a real scare, as we had at times been walking within 30 meters of a trail. Now we would have to stay still further away from any trails.

Looking back on that day, I realized that while we had really stirred up the NVA when we killed the Chinese officers, all we had really accomplished was to greatly increase their security efforts in the area. At the rate things were going, we would need a little luck to get out of the area cleanly. We still had over 4 kilometers to go to get to the nearest LZ for extraction.

I backed up into our security circle, and quietly explained my concerns to the senior Green Beret. He was very unhappy with this turn of events, and said it might take us two more nights to get to the LZ. We would have to move even more slowly than we were moving, just to be able to avoid potential Booby-traps or ambushes.

We stayed hidden until 1930 then moved out going the opposite direction from the trail. When we got to the top of the ridge, we went about 20 meters further over the ridge then turned back toward our extraction LZ.

At 2240 we saw another patrol, and went to ground. This patrol was serious. They were working both sides of the valley in skirmish lines. Each line contained 10 or 11 soldiers. They were working along the hill, with a spread of about 2 meters between each man in the line.

They were moving slowly, and then would stop and listen for

about 30 seconds. They would they move forward about 20 meters, stop and repeat the process.

At the rate they were going, we had about 5 or 6 minutes to get away. I signaled everyone to crawl back up and over the hill. The point man and I were not quite over the hill, when the patrol reached a point about 40 meters away.

I knew that we did not have enough cover to get over the hill without being seen. I crawled under the largest bush I could get under, and pulled out two grenades to throw when they got closer. The point man had watched me, and did the same thing. I straightened the pins in the grenades and got ready to throw.

Suddenly shouting came from the other half of the patrol, and the patrol squad on our side of the valley turned and moved quickly to join the other group of NVA. I pushed the pins back in the grenades and bent them.

I motioned to the point man to crawl over the hill. After about 2 or 3 minutes I crawled after him. We both got over without being seen, and pulled in close with the rest of our men. I suggested that we needed to go into the area that had just been patrolled by the group on the other side of the hill.

It took about 15 minutes to get behind the patrolling NVA soldiers, then we quietly moved out down into the area that the patrol had just come through.

At 0100 I pulled us into a security position, and told them that I thought that we had to find a way to get to the extraction point before 0300. We could then call in to get an extraction.

The team was worried that we would be seen moving too fast. I pointed out that if we stayed where we were, we were going to be found anyway. I told the point man to move out, and we began to move again.

Twice in the next two hours we had to avoid more patrols. As soon as they would pass, we would move into the area that had just patrolled and continue to move as quickly as we could while maintaining silence.

At 0345, we reached a point about 100 meters from the extraction LZ. We called in for extraction, and were told that we would be picked up about 0600. We acknowledged the pickup time, and then prepared for a security sweep of the area around the LZ.

Two members of the team would move around the LZ keeping a distance of about 30-40 meters away from the clear area. They would circle the entire site, looking for enemy troops. When the team returned, they had found 2 pairs of trail watchers observing the LZ.

We would need to remove this threat by killing them, and it had to be done with no noise and completed at least 30 minutes prior to the expected extraction.

I opened my pack, and pulled out my 22 berretta pistol and silencer. Once assembled, I had a member of the scout team lead me back to the nearest pair of trail watchers.

When we got to the first location, I continued to crawl toward the enemy soldiers, and the guide prepared to fire his AK-47 if something went wrong. I finally got to within about 20 feet, took aim, and double tapped (shot the target twice) the soldier sitting down. Then I moved my aim to the other soldier, and double tapped him also.

I waited about a minute for any noise or response then I crawled out to the two soldiers. One was dead, but the other was moaning softly. I took no chance and shot him once again in the head.

I crawled back to the guide, and we moved off toward the other pair of trail watchers. By the time I had a good visual on them, it was 0500, and daylight would be coming soon.

I crawled in toward the two trail watchers and repeated the process I had used on the first pair. We now had a secure LZ, unless some more soldiers or a patrol showed up. We moved off and rejoined the rest of our team.

At 0555 we received a call from the chopper that it was 3 or 4 minutes out. They asked that I throw smoke to identify.

I waited about 1 minute, then threw out a red smoke grenade into the clear area of the LZ. The chopper acknowledged red smoke and began to land. As they were coming down, we started running toward the chopper. He landed about 15 feet from the smoke, and we all jumped in.

The pilot immediately lifted off, and started exiting the area at a height that just cleared the trees. We were over two miles away before we started gaining altitude. When we got to about 4000 feet, we all took a deep breath, and began to relax. It was quiet the rest of the way home. We landed at Nakhon Phanom about 0815.

I sent my team to get cleaned up, and have some chow. I jumped in a jeep that was waiting for me and was driven to the TOC for the debriefing. After debriefing, I went and cleaned up, then stopped at the team tent and shook hands with each man. I told them that if it was OK with them, the next time we worked together, how about a nice quiet ambush. They all laughed, and I walked out.

The jeep took me to the C-130. I flew back to Kimpo in Korea. I was still naïve and inexperienced enough to hope that all my missions would not be this tough. We all have hopes, but events seldom happen as you wish.

This hard lesson would be burned into my mind over the next 8 months **Inside the World of Mirrors**.

Chapter 2
Gate Keeper on the Ho Chi Mein Trail

I landed in Cambodia at Nakhon Phanom late in the afternoon. I had come in from Korea to "Plan" another mission, this time into Laos. It wasn't the first time I had been here, and it probably wouldn't be the last time.

The place still had its unique "perfume". Every country in this part of the world has a distinctive smell. If you blindfolded me, set me down in Cambodia, Korea, Laos, Hong Kong, or North Vietnam, I could probably tell you where we were.

The bombing of North Vietnam had not yet started, and the "Powers That Be" wanted to know what the traffic count was on the Ho Chi Mein trail. A number of teams had gone in to try to accomplish this mission, but were torn every time they set up. It seemed that a sniper would hit them within 4 or 5 hours after they had set up.

The sniper's fire immediately alerted the heavy concentration of NVA in the area, and the teams had a difficult time trying to get out. Almost 50% of the teams were KIA (Killed in Action) or WIA (Wounded in Action).

The briefing team wanted to know if I could go in and take out the sniper. I told them that there was virtually no chance that I could find the sniper. They persisted in their request for me to go after the sniper. After repeating the word "NO" at least five more times, it became apparent that I would have go through a lengthy and tiresome process to prove to them that it just wasn't possible.

The only chance that I saw was to pick a location for a team to setup in that had only one or two good lines of fire for the sniper. I would need to setup with my security team in a place that would give me a good line of fire on the potential sniper sights. I was positive trying to find such a location was a waste of time, but was just something I had to go through.

We called for the Imagery Photos of a complete group of grid squares on the map showing the area of interest.

It took about 6 tedious hours to narrow down the potential to two sites. One would have two excellent sniper line-of-sight positions, and the other would have three positions. After further study, I determined that there was no way to cover all the second site's three sniper positions. In addition, at the first site, I could cover one position well, but was blocked out of the second position.

I finally told the MCO that it was not a practical mission. It was because of the probability of not having a clean line-of-sight, and therefore having the need to move to an alternate position which was a dangerous activity.

A sniper does not want to have to move, because movement makes you a target. I highly preferred to find the target, not be the target.

They told me that they badly needed the traffic count showing numbers and times of day when the traffic was heaviest. I then suggested that they gather the information in a slightly different manner. My proposal was based on the size of the mission teams that had been in before.

The smallest team they had sent out had 5 team members, and it was hard to move that many people through the bush without being seen or heard if you were working in an area that was heavily manned by the enemy.

I proposed that only a two man team go in. The infiltration would be slow and difficult, but could probably be done over a two or three night period. With the smaller size of the team, it would dramatically reduce the potential of being seen or found.

The two man team would then need to observe the traffic and timing for 2 or 3 days. Then the exfiltration would take another two or three days.

I suggested that the team take a radio that would broadcast for a maximum of about 10 miles line of site. This would be a weak signal, and therefore be more difficult for the NVA to try to triangulate the broadcast location. In the worse case, a team member could talk to the FAC on duty by climbing a tall tree if necessary.

I suggested that they use the best man on point they had, to help make infiltration successful. I was told that a local from the hill people named Phaun was the best around. In addition, he spoke broken but passable English.

I asked them who they had to send out on the mission with Phaun. They went away to find out who would go with Phaun. The next morning they returned to me, and said they were not comfortable sending one of their people into the brush with only a local guide. What they were really saying was none of their people wanted to run the mission.

Then they told me that they wanted me to take the mission. When you get SIO personnel that don't want to go on a mission, you know that it will be extremely difficult and highly dangerous. By their standards, they were telling me that as far as they were concerned, I was expendable because they were not responsible for me. That's exactly what you get when you are the poor sucker that comes up with the plan.

I went to meet Phaun. He was about 4'10" tall, and tough as a nail. I learned that his father had been the head man in his village. He had been on a two day trip to buy and sell some items, and when he got back he found the village burned to the ground.

He finally found a few scattered members of the village, and was told that the NVA had come and destroyed everything because his father would not give them rice. The NVA then killed his family. He had worked with the different groups at Nakhon Phanom ever since.

We talked about the mission over the next two hours. I was satisfied that it could be done, so I told the briefer that Phaun and I would run the mission.

The next evening, just before dusk, Phaun and I were dropped in at a cold LZ almost on the border between Laos and Cambodia. We were about 10 kilometers west of the target area. Phaun led us off to the northeast and we covered about 4 Kilometers till we found a good place to hole up for the day.

He had moved through the jungle like a ghost. He made no sound, not even moving a leaf as he worked his way through the brush. I was impressed by his movement skills. Our hide was about 30 meters up a steep slope, in a small cave with good cover in front of it.

The NVA must have heard the helicopter pass by overhead and therefore knew that someone was around, They patrolled all day and late into the evening. We would catch a glimpse of them, or hear them as they passed by, but we were not found.

I was worried that they were going to be setting up ambush positions between us and the trail. Phaun agreed with me, so about 2200 we set out again. This time we went north, not east towards the trail area. Phaun was really good, as he worked us around two different NVA positions without any problems. Around 0300, after covering about 5 kilometers, we turned back to the southeast.

After another hour, I began to become very concerned. The pre-dawn light would be starting in another hour or so, and we needed to be in a solid hide location to rest out the day.

About 0430 we still had not found a good hide, and my anxiety was pumping adrenaline through my system full bore. Phaun said we needed to hide now and pointed straight up at the triple canopy tree we were standing under.

It took a moment for me to understand that he wanted to climb the tree, and get up above the second canopy of leaves. We would have to tie ourselves to the tree, and wait out the day. With no other viable choice, we went up the tree. The second canopy of leaves was about 40-50 feet off the ground, so we went up about 60 feet and tied ourselves in at the junction of several large limbs and the trunk of the tree.

It was not the most comfortable place to wait in, but it turned out to be the safest place. During the day we heard three patrols go right by us and they never looked up.

We had heard truck motors off and on throughout much of the day, so Phaun climbed further up the tree to see if he could get a visual on the movement. To my surprise, he found a place almost at the top of the tree that he could see the crest of a hill about 4 Kilometers away, and the road came right over the crest of the hill.

He came back down, and we talked quietly about just staying

here and watching the road for two more days. It would be tough physically, but offered the best way to get the information without being found.

We took one hour turns going up the tree and watching the road with binoculars. He could not count well, only being able to count to ten, but he could make a mark on a piece of tree bark. A long vertical mark for every 10 trucks, a slash mark was 10 bicycles loaded up and being pushed, and an X shaped notch was 10 NVA soldiers.

In this way, he could keep an accurate count for me, and I would keep the totals in my note book. The time period was noted with the count when I wrote it down each time. By the end of daylight, we had a good count of what had gone by.

I was not surprised that all movement on the road stopped about 30 minutes before dark. The NVA supply chain usually did not move during the night this far north. About 40 miles south of us, they usually moved only at night, and rested during the day because of the absence of the triple canopy jungle.

By the end of the second day, about 1800, I decided that I had spent far too much time in the tree. We even had some solid intelligence. In addition, I wasn't sure that I would be able to walk if we stayed up in the tree much longer. Phaun went down the tree part way to check for movement.

He was back in less than five minutes. He said that a trail watcher had been left behind and was located about 20 meters from the trail about 20 feet from our tree. If he saw any movement, he would fire his rifle, and the NVA would come running to join the party.

Phaun said he could get him with his cross bow, but we would have to go down immediately, carry him off to hide him, and then exfiltrate as quickly as we could.

We packed up, and Phaun went down with his cross bow. In about 5 minutes he came back up and waved me down. It turned out his job had been easy. The trail watcher had been sitting up against a tree half asleep, and now he would never wake up again. We carried him about forty meters further off the trail, dumped him in some heavy brush, and covered him as best we could. Then Phaun led us off toward our extraction point.

It was very slow going because we had to stay well up the hillside away from the trail area. In addition, we had to find any additional trail watchers, so it was move for 30 seconds, then watch and listen for 2 or 3 minutes.

This miserable snail's pace continued all night. It was exhausting to move through brush and make no noise. You felt gingerly with your foot to be sure you were not stepping on a stick or something else that would make noise. Noise at night in the bush is the kiss of death.

We found three more trail watchers. We were able to work around two of them, but had to kill and hide the third one.

About 0330, we got back to the cave we had used the first night. We could go no further, as dawn was approaching.

I told Phaun I would take first watch, and he stretched out to try to get some sleep. He was asleep within two minutes, but shortly thereafter began to snore. I woke him up and had him roll over and sleep on his stomach. It is the best way to sleep in the bush, because you usually didn't snore in this position.

After about 45 minutes, I heard two shots fired from the direction which we had come from. Obviously someone had come to check on the trail watchers, and had discovered one was missing. About 30 minutes later, I heard two more shots. I assumed that they had reached a point in the trail where the other trail watcher was missing. The second pair of shots was much louder than the first pair. That meant that they were working toward us.

We had no choice now. We had to move immediately, as they would be searching both sides of the trail area with large groups of soldiers.

We moved the rest of the morning, fighting exhaustion all the way. We finally each had to take a black bomber, which was a pill of adrenaline enhanced speed, and that is all that allowed us to keep going.

We finally broke free of the search after about 6 hours. We found a deep stand of cane, and crawled inside to rest. We both lay on our stomachs and passed out. Neither one of us could stay alert or awake.

We woke up late in the afternoon. Luck had been with us. We had slept from exhaustion and just laid there for several hours, but had not been found. Sometimes getting lucky is the difference between dead and alive. I figured that we had just used up our ration of luck, so no more taking chances.

I hooked up the radio, and got the FAC on the line. He said he could get us extracted tomorrow morning, but I told him the search was too heavy and we would not last that long. I called him again an hour later, and confirmed a penetrator extraction for 2300.

I had an infrared shielded beacon that they could use to locate us. I went up the tree and set up the beacon tied to a limb at the top of the tree. Five minutes early they radioed for me to confirm they had seen the beacon.

I talked them in to a hover right above us, and they dropped the penetrator down through the jungle trees. We scrambled out and grabbed the penetrator. You sat on the fold down legs on the penetrator and held on to the metal body as you were pulled up.

I hooked Phaun onto the penetrator, and they pulled him up through the trees. It seemed like they had forgotten me, but it was only the adrenaline in my system that was making time seem to move so slow. Within 5 minutes I was on the penetrator and up in the chopper. Two minutes later we were long gone.

We were scratched, bruised, and beaten up by the mission and the extraction, but we were alive. Every time you came back in one piece, it was a good mission.

Back at Nakhon Phanom they were amazed at the count. The traffic was so heavy they decided to call in an "Arc Light" mission.

During an "Arc Light" mission, a flight of B-52 bombers would drop enough bombs, on the target location we gave them, to create a path of destruction about a mile long and ½ mile wide. The result would look like someone had started digging two hundred swimming pools, but had never got around to finishing any of them. No tree would be left standing. It would be total devastation and destruction.

Two days later the mission flew, and the Air Force requested a BDA, (Bomb Damage Assessment). They wanted someone to go back in on the ground, and give them a report on what they had accomplished.

I looked at the briefing officers and said "No Way"! We got out once, and we were not going to push our luck any further.

It was just one more completed mission **Inside the World of Mirrors** that wasn't going to make any real difference in the war. I flew out the next morning back to Korea.

Chapter 3
The Technical Side of War

The annual TET offensive in South Vietnam was finally over. A lot of people had died, and not just soldiers. The civilian casualties were very high also.

The "Intelligence Weenies" back in the states had decided that the reason that this TET was so brutal this time was that the NVA and Viet Cong (VC) had been supplied with a much larger supply of munitions and other war materials. This brilliant analysis led to a decision to interdict the supply chain.

Now you would think that it makes sense that if the enemy has less to fight with, then the enemy will be less effective. It also seems logical to expend time, material, and manpower to make this happen.

What did not make sense was where the interdiction was to take place, and how it was going to happen.

According to the mission statement, a stretch of the Ho Chi Mein trail would be targeted over a 30 mile length. The target area was to be covered by 3 mountain top artillery fire bases.

The target area was covered by thick, tall, triple canopy jungle. In addition, the trail was not a single road as many people believed. In some areas it had as many as three different routes within a 1 mile area.

They wanted to use artillery fire to attack the trail. How do you direct artillery fire to a target you can't see? Aerial surveillance was no good, and you couldn't put observers into the area you were going to blow up.

The technical research group at the farm in Virginia had come up with what they thought was a solution to this type of situation.

They had developed a small piece of equipment that would detect movement through the vibrations in the ground such as trucks or troops would make when they passed by. It had an antenna that looked like a green climbing vine, and could transmit a signal approximately 10 miles. The signal could be picked up by a specially equipped air plane and transmitted to a hill top fire base where the artillery could respond with a fire mission.

This all sounded wonderful back in Washington, but when it came time to implement the program, I was stuck with all the problems.

The first problem was that the device had to be implanted within 10 meters of the trail, and the antenna had to be run up a bush or small tree. That required someone to go in and put these things in place, notate their exact position, setup the antenna, and the get out without being found.

The second problem was getting the exact position calculated. The only way that the Mission Control Officer (MCO), Mike Simmons, had come up with was for a helicopter to fly over the area until we had directed it so that it was above the sensor. The helicopter then could take multiple sight readings on the surrounding mountains, and thus an exact position would be determined.

I knew that this process was going to fail as soon as I heard it. The planting of the sensor system within 10 meters of a constantly busy trail would be almost impossible to accomplish without being seen.

Even if you pulled off the miracle of getting the system put in place and activated, having a helicopter hover over you was a certain way to get every enemy soldier within several miles running to come join to the fun and games. This was a sure and certain method of committing suicide.

The technical issues added more complexity, and further insured that whoever was crazy enough to try to plant the sensor and activate them, using the mission plan, had exactly zero chance of coming out alive. This was another example of a typical "Washington Brain Fart".

I had seen another "technical wonder" a few months earlier. This was a special version of a claymore mine that could be detonated by a remote electronic signal much like a TV remote control.

The problems were that (1) you had to have a clear line of sight to the claymore, and (2) you had to stand directly behind the claymore to use the remote detonator.

Have you ever considered how often you might find a clear open area in the jungle? The answer is of course, you don't. You also had to stand directly behind the claymore to activate it, which put you in the back blast zone.

It was just another example of research creating something that would kill you, even if it didn't get any of the enemy. The sensor mission as written was just another way to get people killed for no purpose or gain.

I made these points extremely clear to the briefing officers, and they went away muttering about stupid grunts. I might be stupid but I wasn't crazy enough to volunteer to commit suicide.

They came back to me the next day, and said that MACV (Military Assistance Command Vietnam) really wanted to give this a try. They asked me how I thought it could be done.

They brought in all the maps with their best guesses where the trails would be. I sat down and studied all the information, then took a break and went over to a marine recon platoon that had worked around the area in question.

I learned that they considered that the enemy was not quite as vigilant as I might expect, because no bombing or artillery missions had ever occurred in the area. They had been in and out near the mission area several times on simple observation missions, and while it was tight and hairy, getting in and out was possible.

"IF" they could get me in and out then one problem was set aside. We talked for over 3 hours, and we finally came up with a way to locate the sensor without using a helicopter.

We would set up radio signal triangulation on 3 mountain tops around the target area. When the sensor was installed, we would radio the FAC and give him a time that the signal was going to be sent. The signal would last 15 seconds. They would get one chance to get an azimuth to the sensor. They would record the azimuth at each site.

By taking the location of each site, and the azimuth to the sensor, we could draw 3 lines on a map that would let us exactly calculate the location of the sensor. Using two sites would probably work, but by using three sites we made it more likely to have a solid detection and location of the signal. We would then move to the next sensor position, and repeat the process.

We had 6 sensor systems, and thought that we could get them installed in two or three nights. The recon marines would take me in, I would do the setup, and then we would come back out. We figured that it would take between 5 and 10 days to get into the area, accomplish the mission profile, and get out.

Two days later, about 30 minutes before dark, I dropped in with the 5 marines from the recon group. Our LZ was about 8 kilometers from the general target area, and turned out to be cold.

We got on the ground safely, and after about 30 minutes, moved out toward the target area. We made good time until about midnight. Then we ran into trail watchers. By 0200 we had worked around two of them, and were starting to look for a place to hide during the day.

We moved further up the side of the mountain, and found a dense brushy area. We set out 4 claymores, and designated our emergency exfiltration route and meeting point.

We lay down in a circle with our feet on the inside of the circle and about 3 feet apart. We set up string tied between each of us so that the man on watch could silently alert the others if he saw something he considered dangerous.

We had pulled brush from an area about 200 meters away, and used it to further camouflage our position. The area was busy all day, with a lot of NVA soldiers passing by.

We were keeping track of the traffic volume, and had seen over 200 enemy combatants pass by. In addition, just before dark, a group stopped about 100 meters from us, and started hanging up hammocks to sleep in.

With the enemy so close, we could not move out until almost 2200. We pulled back our claymores, and began the really slow movement necessary to get away from their camp area, but by midnight we were clear and moving toward the target area again.

About 0400 we found another good hide, and set up again to spend the day. This time we were over 300 meters from the trail. The day passed much like yesterday, but this time we didn't have anyone stop near us as evening approached.

We broke camp about 2000 and started our final approach to the target area. We had a visual on a well used trail by 0130, so we set up a protective overwatch position, and I moved down near the trail. I had the sensor set up under a heavy bush, and the antenna was stretched up into the limbs of the bush.

I signaled our radio operator, and he called the FAC. The FAC alerted the three signal location sites, and then called to say they were ready. I was signaled by the radio operator to push the transmit button, and I held it down for a count of 15. I started moving back away from the trail when the radio operator signaled that each of the 3 listening stations had got the signal.

We pulled back up the hill and began to move toward the next position. We got to our next sensor position about 0330 and went through the setup and signal process again. Once again we got a good response from the FAC and I had started to pull back away from the trail. Suddenly I got the warning signal from the marine nearest to me.

I immediately went to ground and crawled behind some bushes. I had barely got under the bush when I heard people talking. It was a NVA patrol, but they were very casual about their activities. If they hadn't been talking, I probably would have been seen, and the mission would have turned very ugly.

They walked by and continued on up the trail. They had walked within about 20 meters of me. The adrenaline in my system was pounding and my nerves were stretched tight. After they were out of sight, I crawled about 20 meters into heavier brush, slowly stood up, and continued up the hillside to our meeting point.

We had a quick conference, and decided to find a hide and hole up again for the day. At 0430 we found a thick patch of cane, and carefully crawled inside it.

No extra camouflage was used, as we had no time to collect it and build it into the stand of cane. By 0630 the traffic on the trail was going strong. During the day we counted over 250 more NVA marching south on the trail.

Sometimes you just get a feeling that everything is going far too smooth. For some reason I was getting very nervous. My adrenaline was beginning to pump me up. I had to take some time to try to get myself under control again. If you are all juiced up in the bush, then mistakes will happen. You have to maintain a high alertness level without getting jumpy.

1800 came and went, and we were preparing to move again. The outer watch position signaled more traffic was coming, so we went down in the bush again. This was no troop movement this time. This was a serious patrol, with flankers out about 20 meters on both sides of the trail. They would move about 20 meters, then stop and listen. They were working both sides of the trail.

At the rate they were moving, they would find us in the next 30 minutes. We had no choice. We had to move now. We couldn't stand up, as they would be able to see us, so we started crawling up the hill as quietly as we could.

It was in a very steep area when "Defecation Hit the Cooling Apparatus". One of the marines was crossing an area where there were some loose stones. His foot slipped on some small stones and started a mini-avalanche down the side of the hill. This attracted the patrols attention immediately, and they came running toward us firing their weapons.

I shouted out the word "REBOUND". This was our emergency signal. Upon hearing this, three of the marines jumped up and went running up the hill, while the remaining marines and I flipped our weapons to full auto and blasted away at the patrol.

The three members that had started running went about 20 meters, ducked down, and began to fire on the patrol. The other marines and I then jumped up and ran till we were past the marines currently firing. We then went down, and started firing, and they started running.

We did this for about 60 meters till we got to the top of the hill. One of the marines had taken a slug along the left side of his chest, just gashing the flesh enough to make it bleed heavily. So far, the rest of us had not been hit.

Once we got over the top of the hill I yelled "SCATTER". This was our code word for splitting into 2 groups. Then, we each threw 2 grenades over the hill top, and took off running. We had an emergency meeting point that we had designated when we setup in the cane.

One group of 3 would run off to the left through the bush, and the other group would run off to the right through the bush. You don't run on a trail unless you are ready to die. All we were doing was running as fast as we could to try to get separation from the patrol. The wounded marine was in my group.

About 5 minutes later we heard a massive set of explosions, and heavy fire coming from the direction that the other team of 3 had run. They had probably run into another group of NVA that was setup in an ambush position. The high level of fire continued for about 30 seconds and then stopped.

My group of three was still trying to clear the area. Our progress had slowed down because the wounded marine was starting to have trouble keeping up. I told the two marines to keep running, and I stopped and set up two claymores with timers on them.

I stuck one in the ground with a 2 minute timer, and took off running with the other still in my hand. About 100 meters later, I stuck the second claymore in the ground and set a 4 minute timer. Then I was off running again.

We had run far enough that we had gone down the hill and through the low area. We were starting to go up hill again. I caught up with the two marines. The wounded marine was being helped by his partner, and I grabbed his other arm to help and we took off again.

Just then the first claymore timers went off and we heard screams. We had obviously got somebody's attention, and maybe that would slow them down enough for us to find a way to disappear.

Just as we reached the top of the hill, the second timed claymore went off. We went running over the top of the hill and ran right into a small patrol heading up the hill.

We surprised them and started firing first. The two groups were not more than 30 feet apart, and all three of us fired a full clip into the patrol. Then I threw a WP (White Phosphorous) grenade into the middle of what was left of the patrol. It exploded and we took off again, this time almost carrying the wounded marine.

When I looked down at the wounded marine, I saw he had been

shot again. This time the bullet had gone through his jaw. He looked up and me, tried to say something, choked, and died. I tore off his dog tags, looked at his partner, and said "Just two of us now". We took off running again.

I heard the sound of a dog barking, and knew how much more trouble we were now in. If they were using a dog to track us, running would not do any good. We had to disappear. As we ran down the hill, we came to a small stream.

We jumped in the stream and started wading downstream as fast as we could go. This seemed to go on forever. Then I realized that the sound of the dog was not getting closer.

They must have reached the creek, and figured out that we had gone up or down stream, but they didn't know which way. We kept moving until I saw a stand of cane and reeds in the edge of the creek.

I stopped and cut down two pieces of cane about 2 feet long. I cut it between the joints, because this part of the cane was usually like a tube. Sure enough, they were hollow. I pushed the marine into the bed of reeds, gave him a piece of cane, and said get under water and breathe through the cane. I told him to stay in the reeds and remain underwater till I came back and got him. I then moved about 50 feet downstream to another set of reeds, and did the same thing I told him to do.

After about 20 minutes, I slowly came back up to the surface in the middle of the patch of reeds. I heard a patrol going by on the other side of the creek, so I ducked back down for a few more minutes. When I came back up again, it was quiet.

After about 20 minutes more, I quietly worked my way back to where I had left the last marine. He wasn't there! I searched the immediate area but couldn't find any trace of him. After about 10 minutes, I gave up and started humping back toward our extraction LZ. I was hurting and gasping for breath, but I kept moving.

If I could get back to the extraction LZ, by our last planned extraction time at day light in two days, I could contact the FAC with a small emergency air force pilot's radio. I always carried one in the bush, because you never knew when you would lose the primary radio. Now I would find out if it would really work. If it didn't, then I had a 20 kilometer hike to the nearest fire base.

At 0330 I finally found a good hide on the side of a sharp slope. I knew how much trouble I was in. I had nobody to keep watch while I slept and nobody to work with. If I was found, it was over. I might go to sleep, and never wake up. There were at least 2000 or 3000 NVA between me and the nearest fire base, so walking out was not an option I wanted to try to use.

At this point the adrenaline rush was over. I was exhausted. I just lay down on my stomach, and passed out. It was 2000 when I finally woke up again. I had been asleep over 15 hours, and I was soaked to the skin. It had rained and stormed, and I hadn't even known it.

The good thing about the rain was that it would erase any scent that the dogs could use to track me. The bad thing was that it made me so cold that I was literally shaking in my boots. The only way I could get warm, was to move again.

I was weak and stressed out, but reasonably alert, so I took a deep breath, and worked my way about half way down the slope. I moved all night. Move 20 or 30 feet, then stop and listen. I repeated this till about 0400 when I found another good hide position.

The day passed without incident. At 2100 I moved out again. I was only about 1 kilometer from the extraction LZ. I checked my watch, and it was about time for the FAC to be listening for us to call for extraction.

I clicked on the radio, and to my surprise, in spite of being soaked in the creek, and by the rain storm, it still worked. It was the first thing that had gone right in two days. I swore to myself to never say anything bad about the air force again. I called 3 times before the FAC responded. I quickly told him that an emergency extraction was necessary. He went off to make arrangements for a chopper.

While I waited for his call back, I checked out the LZ. I circled it twice, and found nothing. The FAC called back and said a chopper was on the way and would arrive at the LZ at 0600. It would come down and hover for 1 minute, and if I didn't get on it by then, I would have to walk home.

At 0555 the FAC called me and said the chopper would be at the LZ in 3 or 4 minutes. I confirmed that I was ready, and moved out of the deep brush to the edge of the clearing. Right on time I heard the sound of the chopper.

It came down and hovered about 50 feet away from me. I went running toward the helicopter with my AK-47 raised above my head. I got to the chopper and jumped in. I almost slid through the passenger cabin and out the other door. I grabbed a door frame and held on as we took off.

I slowly pulled myself back inside the chopper. By this time we were gaining altitude and leaving behind the nightmare of the last 2 days.

The door gunner handed me a helmet with an intercom wire, and said the pilot needed to talk to me. I put on the helmet and the pilot asked where the rest of the team was.

All I could do was say I had one dog tag on a KIA (killed in action), and hadn't laid eyes on the other members for some time. Then I thanked him for making the pickup at the LZ under such strange and difficult circumstances. He said "No Problem, glad to see you back."

About an hour and forty-five minutes later the door gunner leaned over and told me we were about 5 minutes out. We landed, and I got out.

I was surprised that there was a jeep waiting for me. I got in and we headed for the TOC. They had a medic there that checked me out. I was scratched up, and had a lot of blood stains on my clothes. He thought I was badly wounded.

I told him I had not been shot. The blood belonged to a fellow team member and gave him the dog tags.

They took me down to the mess hall, and I ate the first real food I had seen in two days. I was starved, exhausted, and very weak. The medic took me to the latrine where I cleaned up, and then took me back to the TOC. I gave them about 30 minutes of a preliminary debriefing and then was led off to a room with a real bed. I crashed on the bed and went to sleep.

When I woke up, I was totally confused as to where I was. I wandered out of the room and found the medic. After talking for a few minutes, I found out that I had slept for over 15 hours. I got my wits about me, ate a large meal, and we went back to the TOC for a full mission debriefing.

During the debriefing, I asked if the two sensors we had planted were working. I was informed that one was completely dead, and the other was had a very weak signal.

We discussed what the problem could be, and the technician that had delivered the equipment to me said that the batteries that ran the equipment were not in a sealed waterproof compartment. The rain storm that had occurred while I was asleep had probably caused them to short out. He said no one had thought to make the battery cases waterproof. After all, the testing was done in Nevada in the desert where it almost never rained.

I got really upset over this information. We had just lost five men to plant a device that would quit working when it got wet. It was wet all the time in the areas we worked in.

Two days later I flew out to the U.S. via Guam. I never did get over losing 5 men for a piece of equipment that could never work long enough to be of use. It wasn't the first time the "Powers That Be" had messed me up because of something stupid, and unfortunately, it wouldn't the last time either.

Upon my arrival back in the U.S., I was immediately taken to the Farm in Virginia. I made it very clear how upset I was with the mission, and the results. After the meeting was over, I told them that I was going to take a break. I left word where they could get a message to me, and said I'd be back in about a week.

With the mood I was in no one raised any objection to my leaving. I left without another word. I swore that the next idiot that wanted to send me out on a mission with new equipment would not like the response he would get. Sometimes even I got to occasionally raise a little hell **Inside the World of Mirrors.**

Chapter 4
A Political Errand

Nakhon Phanom still smelled the same way it had the last time I landed there. I was beginning to associate the smell with trouble, and I was sure that this trip in would be no different. It was late in the afternoon, so I went over to the unofficial club to steal a couple of beers. The nicest thing about the club was that they had a real ice machine. The beer and liquor were cold.

Mike Simmons, the MCO, was sitting in his usual place, in the only recliner in Cambodia. Nobody knew how he got it brought in, but Mike liked his comforts. The rest of us just went with the flow and got what we could out of his little world.

I picked up a beer, and walked over to a table about 3 feet from the recliner, pulled up a chair, and sat down. My first words were direct and to the point. "What Bullshit have you dreamed up this time?"

He grinned and told me that this would be an interesting hike. I would get to meet a lot of new people, though they might not be overly friendly, and if I was lucky, I might leave a mark on them to commemorate my visit.

I just shook my head, and lit a cigarette to go with my beer. After a couple of drinks we called it quits, and he took me over to my room. I knew it was not going to be an easy mission when I saw the air conditioner in the window. I only got good treatment when the mission was going to be ugly.

I met him at the TOC at 1000 the next morning. Mike didn't like to push things by getting up to early. The extra sleep I got was okay with me too. We went into the map room, pulled a file out of his desk, and began the mission overview.

It seemed that there was this NVA political officer in Cambodia that was a bit over zealous in his activities. The local population had learned to be quiet and do as they were told.

Someone in intelligence had code named this officer and his group "Red Poppy". If he didn't get his way, the things could get really ugly.

He travelled with a security group of 10 to 12 soldiers, and would arrive in a village about the time the sun was disappearing behind the mountains. His lectures would last for 3 or 4 hours. If the villagers were attentive and he was in a good mood, he would only take about half their rice, and leave. If he was unhappy, then people died in a very slow and ugly way. His security team seemed to enjoy using the females of the village as a recreation tool.

He was fairly consistent in his time between visits which were usually about every two weeks or so. MACV wanted pictures of what he was doing so they could prove that the NVA and Viet Cong were not the revolutionary friends of the people that they claimed to be.

I just stared at him for a moment and asked if I was supposed to be his camera man? He laughed and said that one of the Green Beret personnel going with me would take the pictures. He just wanted me to take the political officer and his people out when it was over.

I looked him straight in the eye and told him that I was not going to stand there and watch while he and his team had their fun. People would get hurt, or even worse, when the political officer got out of hand.

Mike said to read this mission statement, and make sure you understand it completely. You will do exactly what it says. I'm not going to deal with the backlash from the MACV brass if you don't.

I read the mission statement, and told him to stick it where the sun doesn't shine. He then handed me a tape recorder, and said that it would make things much clearer.

I recognized the voice on the tape immediately. Woody Woodford, a man from "An Organization that Didn't Exist (Hereafter referred to as the shop)," was a southern gentleman with the accent to match. Woody explained that somebody from MACV had convinced the White House that these pictures would really hurt the enemy. It was approved "at the highest level" and that he knew that I would get the job done. He said good luck, and that was the end of the tape. Now I was supposed to be some stupid politician's errand boy.

I just got up and walked out and went to the club. About a half bottle of scotch later, Mike came wandering in. The only other person there was a mechanic, and he waved him out. Then he sat down and asked when I was going to be sober enough to get on with the job. I glared at him, picked up the bottle, and walked out to my room.

The next morning, I staggered over to the mess hall, and drank enough coffee to float a battleship. I knew that I had no choice. I ate a large meal then went to Mike's map room.

I asked him who the team was that was going to go in with me. He picked up the phone, and about 10 minutes later, 5 green berets walked in. I was introduced to them, and we all sat down to work out a plan. We had a rough idea of the schedule and when he was expected to be in a particular area, but no solid timing.

The senior team sergeant suggested that we just pick a site he hit about 10 days ago, and go setup and wait for him. Nothing else could really be done with any certainty.

I suggested that we expand that idea by splitting into two teams. Team 1 would go to the site already picked. Team 2 would go to the nearest village around the Team 1 site. A little time in the map room showed that the nearest village was about 3 kilometers away from the Team 1 site.

We set up radio frequencies, reporting times, and an LZ suitable for both villages. This required that a second camera be used. When Red Poppy showed at either village, a radio contact would be made to the other team. The other team then would move to join the locating team's position.

Three kilometers was normally about a 2 hour trip, but because of the known areas, we could pre-plan non-trail patterns to reach the other site quicker than we normally would do. We could probably cut it to 45 minutes if we absolutely had to.

We planned for a week in the field. This required more ammo, food, an extra radio, and other equipment and supplies than we normally would carry. I would be carrying two shoulder fired weapons. The Green Berets understood the AK-47, but looked at me a little strangely when they saw the other weapon. It was a 22 caliber

Winchester with a standard scope, an infrared scope, and a silencer. In addition, I would be using sub-sonic rounds in it. As usual, I also had my silenced berretta in my pack.

We decided on hitting the LZ about 30 minutes after dawn. That would require that we be at the helicopter pad and loaded up by about 0330. We would go in tomorrow morning. The senior Green Beret and I broke up the teams by skill sets, and each team went off to get ready, and to get some sleep.

I could tell that everyone was ready when we met at the helicopter pad. We were all there about 20 minutes early. We loaded up and took off to the LZ. Our insertion at the LZ was exactly on time. The helicopter had previously made three fake landings at other LZs, to confuse the observation posts and trail watchers where we were inserting. In addition, the helicopter would make two more fake landings after dropping us off to further increase the enemy's confusion.

It must have worked as we landed in a cold LZ. By the time we were out of the LZ and in the bushes, the helicopter was long gone. We waited about 5 minutes, to be sure, then moved further into the bush. At 0600, the two teams split and headed out for their respective observation points.

By 0930 both teams were in deep cover, and did a radio check. We had an excellent observation position on a hill across a small valley from the village for which we were responsible.

We were about 300 meters away from our village. Each one of us would watch the village for two hours then turn it over to the next person. We had a string tied between us to use as a silent warning if something started happening. The day passed without any action involving Red Poppy.

The villagers went about their daily work in the fields, and as dusk arrived, they returned to the village where the women were preparing a meal.

By 2200, Red Poppy had not shown up at either of our observation points. We did a radio check and settled in for a long night of watching the village. At 0500, we did another radio check with the other team. The night had passed without the appearance of Red Poppy.

When we were on watch our total attention was on the village and the area immediately surrounding our hide. When we were off watch, we ate, cleaned our weapons, and slept.

We had a hole dug about 10 feet away in deep brush that we were using as the latrine. All day we took our turns on watch, but saw no sight of our quarry. The 1500 radio check confirmed that the other team had not seen Red Poppy either.

At 1715, the other team contacted us, and gave a "Hot Zone" warning. That was a warning that NVA personnel had been seen approaching the village they were watching.

We immediately packed up, covered the latrine, and began to move toward the other village. By 1900, we were set up on the opposite side of the village from the other team. A quiet radio check indicated that pictures were being taken, but nothing bad had started happening yet.

The villagers had been gathered together, and were sitting on the ground listening to what appeared to be the leader and political officer of Red Poppy. The rest of Red Poppy personnel were positioned in a circle around the villagers. The voice of the speaker was easily heard at our position. I didn't know what he was saying, but the tone of his speech didn't sound threatening.

About 30 minutes into our observation, two villagers got up and went with 2 members of Red Poppy away from the fire toward the back of the village. They returned in a few minutes with what appeared to be two large bags of rice, and set them down in front of the speaker.

The speaker started yelling at the villagers. Apparently he was unhappy with the amount of rice he was being given. Two of his soldiers walked into the group of villagers, and dragged an old man and woman out in front of the villagers.

The soldiers began beating on the old man, continuing to yell and make aggressive movements around the villagers. Then they began to beat on the old woman.

I picked up the radio and quietly called the other team. I said it was time to move in and take them out. The Green Beret leading the other team thought that we should wait. I told him he could wait all he wanted, but that my team was going in to take out Red Poppy. The team leader of the other group said we didn't have the type of pictures he was supposed to get. I told him that he had all he was going to get and that we were moving in.

By the time we had reached a distance of about 30 meters from the village, the political officer had pointed to a young girl in the crowd of villagers. Two of his men went over and yanked her to her feet.

They slapped her around for a minute or two then tore her clothes off. The villagers were murmuring but couldn't do anything with 8 or 9 AK-47s pointed at them.

I motioned for my two team mates to move about 10 meters away from me on either side. While they were moving to the new positions, I got my 22 caliber rifle out, mounted the silencer and scope, and had a good sight picture on the political officer.

By this time, the girl was on the ground, and one of the NVA soldiers was holding her down. Another had unbuttoned his trousers, and was kneeling down between the girl's legs.

I changed my mind, and move my aim to the man between the girl's legs. I fired a round and struck the kneeling soldier in the head knocking him over to the left of the girl. The NVA were confused for a moment.

With the silencer and sub-sonic ammunition, you couldn't hear the sound of my shot if you were 20 feet away from me. I immediately moved my aim to the leader and shot him in the center of his chest.

The remaining NVA soldiers suddenly figured out what was happening, and started looking around to find out where the firing was coming from. At this point the rest of my team took the soldiers under fire. Three more went down within 30 seconds.

The rest of the NVA soldiers ran into the middle of the group of villagers, and immediately grabbed one to act as a hostage to protect them from being shot.

By this time, the other team of Green Berets had moved in close enough to start firing. Since their weapons were AK-47s, the enemy soldiers were confused and turned their hostages toward the sound of the firing. The villagers were busy trying to scramble away from the insanity that had entered their lives.

The NVA had turned toward the sound of firing. They were almost directly sideways to me. I carefully took aim, and put a round into one of the soldiers. The others then began dragging their hostages with them toward the jungle behind the village.

When they reached the jungle, they pushed their hostages down, and took off running into the thick brush. Both teams continued to fire in their direction but did not bring any of the remained NVA down.

We moved around to the back of the village, but the NVA were out of sight by this time. The villagers had all scrambled into their huts. We merged the two teams, and set up two sentry positions at the edge of the brush in the direction that the NVA had run.

The rest of the team went back to the village and started helping the villagers. Three of the villagers had been shot during the attack, and we went to them to try to help.

We radioed in to the FAC and told him that we needed reinforcements and medical personnel for the villagers. We managed to save one of the villagers that had been shot, but the two others died while we tried to help them.

We went from hut to hut till we found the old man they had been beating. One of the Green Berets was fluent enough to get him to understand that we were there to protect him. He went with us from hut to hut and helped calm down the villagers.

I was worried that the NVA would try to come back and attack us like we had attacked them. The radio man said the choppers were on the way, and would be here in about 2 hours. They were bringing medical personnel, and an additional squad of soldiers to help increase security.

I left the senior Green Beret in charge in the village, and went to each of the sentry positions. I let them know that I was going to make a sweep around the camp about 30 meters out, and see if I could find anything. I told them to be sure it wasn't me if they started shooting. I then moved off in the direction that the NVA run.

I would move four or five feet, stop and listen, then move again. After I got out about 30 meters I got down and started to crawl. I moved about 30 feet this way then stopped and waited. After about 10 minutes, I heard a rustle in the bushes about 20 feet to my right.

I had my AK-47 loaded and ready, but could not see who or what was causing the noise. I aimed my weapon in the general direction of the noise, and froze in place. I was barely breathing. It was now a game where the first person to move or be seen would be the loser.

When you are in the bush at night, you can't really see anything clearly. But if you stared at a single point, like a tree, your peripheral vision would pick up movement that you would otherwise not notice.

I caught something moving out of the corner of my eye. I didn't move or change position. The waiting game continued for what seemed like forever, till I saw a shadow beside a bush move.

I very slowly moved my aim to the shape, and fired three quick shots. The shadow went down and disappeared. I didn't move because movement in this situation was an invitation to a visit from the grim reaper.

I heard some sounds coming from the area where I had fired, but never saw anything again. I waited for almost 30 minutes before I slowly got up, and began to back away from where I had fired. I didn't hear or see anything more as I worked my way back to the village.

About the time I got back to the village, I could hear the sound of the choppers coming in. There were three choppers, and each had to wait while one landed, then took off again as the landing area for them was very small. The first to come in brought the squad of infantry soldiers to give us more fire power and additional security. The medical people were the last to land.

An interpreter came in with the medical personnel. He began to talk to the old man, and was soon getting a good response from him. It was now about an hour to sunrise, and the interpreter kept going from hut to hut talking to the villagers.

By 0600 he had convinced the old man, who was the village chief that the villagers needed to come back to a safe area with us. He told the villagers that the NVA would be back, and that to stay meant to die.

The village chief was promised food and shelter for all his people if they would come with us. By 1100, we had choppers coming in and leaving with the villagers. By 1500 the only people left were the squad of infantry and me. It took another 2 hours before we were picked up and headed back to the compound.

When we landed I went to see Mike Simmons. He was sitting

in his recliner, a drink in one hand, and a cigar in the other. He had already talked to two of the Green Berets and was highly amused by my use of a 22 caliber silenced Winchester. He asked me why I would carry such a light weight weapon into the bush.

I just looked at him and shook my head. I went over and got a beer. I came back, sat down, and lit a cigarette. I told him that if he was so stupid to not understand the value of a silenced weapon with sub-sonic ammunition, then he needed to be replaced. He started laughing, and lifted his glass in a toast to me.

I felt pretty good about the mission. We had erased Red Poppy as an effective instrument for the NVA. I felt sorry for the villagers. They had lived at the village for many generations. Now they had nothing. The people in charge of resettlement supposedly would take care of them, but it would never be the same.

I got up and went out the door to talk to the chopper crews. They said the villagers were at a resettlement facility now. I thanked them for everything they had done.

After a cold shower, some chow, and clean clothes, I felt better about what had occurred. In the great scheme of things as the war was going, what had happened amounted to exactly nothing. But to me, it was one of the few missions that I felt had made a real difference.

The villagers were alive, and that was good enough for me. It was a far better ending than I was used to having **Inside the World of Mirrors.**

Chapter 5
The Ghost of Hill 328

I was beginning to wonder why they didn't just leave me at Nakhon Phanom. I seem to spend more time running back and forth than I did actually working in Korea.

This assignment could make me a legend in my own mind. When a firebase is getting mortared almost every night, why do they need me to make the NVA go away? They could handle themselves in South Vietnam just fine. Now they had put their first firebase in Cambodia, and they didn't know how to take care of the problem.

The Captain at the fire base had complained to his superior. This process made its way up the chain of command and eventually came back down and landed in Mike Simmons lap at Nakhon Phanom.

Mike must have spent half his time figuring out crazy things for me to do. This time he wanted me to go in and take out the VC mortar teams with a silenced 22 caliber Winchester that I had used before on some of the missions I had run for him.

Now I was supposed to go into a fire base by chopper. No one but the commanding officer was allowed to know what I was doing. I asked Mike how he came up with this little trip for me, and he said he remembered how effective I had been with the use of silenced weapons.

His goal was to make the NVA confused about how they were losing their mortar teams. He figured that if strange things kept happening to the mortar teams, then they would stop using them.

We talked it over for about 3 hours, and came up with a plan. I would wear a Ghilli Suit. A Ghilli was a special piece of outer ware, made with pieces of vegetation laced into a net mesh that makes the wearer blend in with the terrain so as to be virtually invisible. My face and hands would be camouflaged also. In effect, I would be a shadowy bush that no one would notice.

By using the silenced weapons and subsonic ammunition, the NVA would not know who or what was doing the damage. When they lost enough personnel and equipment, maybe they would stop mortaring the fire base.

I got my equipment and supplies all together, and after a couple of drinks with Mike at the club, I went to bed early to get a solid night of sleep in preparation for the mission.

Late the next morning I boarded a chopper and off we went. About 1300 I landed at the fire base which was at a location designated as Hill 328. I ignored all the troops and walked straight to the command bunker. The Captain in charge was out, so I sent the radio man to tell him he had a visitor.

When the Captain came in, he waved the radio operator out to another bunker, and sat down. He just stared at me for about 30 seconds, then lit a cigar and said "How do you want to do this?"

I asked him for a history of the mortar attacks, and he told me that they always seemed to come from one of three areas. He never knew which place it would come from. He just knew it would come again.

When I queried him about area patrolling around the fire base, he said that he had a patrol go out every night about 1900 to try and find the NVA. His patrols had no success in finding them.

We went over his patrol patterns, and nothing special jumped up and got my attention. I said I would go out with the patrol as the last man in line, but would drop off after we got away from camp. When I was done I would come back in behind the morning patrol. He asked who's going with me. I just looked at him and told him Mr. Winchester and pointed at the bag carrying the carbine. He just shook his head, and marked on a local map the areas that the NVA had used in the past.

I pushed my gear back against the wall, lay back on it, and said wake me up 45 minutes before the patrol goes out. It was best to get some more rest now, as it would be a long night alone in the bush.

He left the bunker, and went over to another small bunker where the radio man had set up.

At 1830 he woke me up, and said that the patrol was forming up now. I pulled my silenced Winchester out of its bag and mounted the night vision scope. I loaded up with my AK-47 in hand and the Winchester strapped across my chest. My silenced 22 berretta was on my pistol belt. The clothes and equipment I had on were totally hidden by the Ghilli Suit. I painted up my face and hands, checked that the tape was still good on all my gear, and went out to go to work.

The Captain told them that I would be following them for a while to observe, but not to worry if I dropped off by myself. The patrol moved out with me last in line. One of the patrol members said something about a "Walking Bush" following them as they left the camp. That description of me in my Ghilli suit would actually seem to be a good description to almost anyone who saw it for the first time.

We went about 600 meters down the trail till I found what I was looking for. A large stand of Elephant Grass was to the left of the patrol area. When no one was looking back, I stepped off into the grass and disappeared.

I moved slowly for about an hour, till I reached a point about 100 meters outside of the normal range for a mortar to be used against the camp. I went to ground in some deep brush.

I spent the night moving slowly around the camp, but no mortar attack occurred. I worked my way to the area just outside the camp where I had been told the patrol usually took a break.

I crawled to within 15 feet of the patrol. When the sergeant leading the patrol said to mount up and get ready to go back in, I spoke up and said mind if I join you. I startled the patrol when I spoke because they had not heard or seen me approach. After a moment of confusion, the sergeant took control of the patrol and we moved out going back up the hill to the firebase.

When we entered the firebase, the Captain came out and motioned me to his bunker. He then started to debrief the patrol. Most of the members of the patrol looked at me as if I was something out of a horror movie. I even heard one say he never heard or saw me. I had just appeared as a bush next to them.

Several times during the day I overheard conversations about me. They usually referred to me as the ghost. I ate, cleaned up, told the captain to wake me up 45 minutes before they were ready to go out in the evening, and went back to sleep.

The Captain woke me up at 1830 again. I ate a quick meal, put on my gear and paint, and went out to follow the patrol out again. This time they were trying to watch for me to leave the patrol. I just lagged far enough back that when the trail took a turn about 500 meters out I was temporarily not in their sight. I simply stepped behind a large tree and sat down. After about 20 minutes, I moved back toward my search area.

About 2200 hours I heard the first mortar pop out of the tube. It was about 200 meters away from me. I moved out slightly away from the fire base and got behind the mortar team's position. Then I slipped back toward them. They only had one man out on security on each side of the tube. I took my Winchester off my chest strap and replaced it with the AK-47.

I crawled to about 20 meters from the first security man and put a round in his head. He dropped like a lead weight. I moved my aim to the other security man and shot him twice in the chest.

The two men manning the tubes had heard nothing. They were intent on feeding the rounds in the tube. I crawled about 15 feet left to get a better angle. Just as the loader was about to drop another round in the tube, I shot him in the head. I immediately moved my aim to his partner and shot him in the head.

I waited for about 15 minutes to make sure there that were no other NVA around, and stood up and walked to the first guard I had shot. I grabbed him and pulled him over to the tube. I laid him out then I lined up the loader and his assistant beside him. I went out, got the last guard, and pull him in beside the others.

I removed a pair of special white phosphorus charges with timers from my pack. I dropped one down the tube, and put the other timed charge in the crate of mortar rounds. Then I walked away. I got back into a good hide position to watch the show.

Ten minutes later the timed charges went off, and everything within 15 meters lit up in flame. The firebase went on full alert when the explosion happened. Flares went up in the sky floating on parachutes. Everyman in the firebase thought a major attack was coming.

After about an hour, I started moving back toward the camp. I worked my way up the hill till I was only about 50 meters from the camp's entry point for the patrol. I crawled up in some heavy bush about 10 feet from the trail and settled in to wait.

About 0500 I heard the patrol coming. They were making all kinds of noise. Metallic sounds from metal on the web gear preceded them as they came up the hill and walked right past me.

I just stood up and walked into camp right behind the last man in the patrol. When the Captain came out to meet the patrol, I just kept on walking to his bunker. The patrol started blaming each other for not knowing I was with them.

I cleaned my weapons, washed up, and sat down to eat. A few minutes later the Captain came in with a grin on his face. He told me that the patrol was all upset that they didn't know I was around.

I just nodded my head and told him that they were a little casual about watching their back trail when they got close to camp. He said he would have a talk with the Sergeants leading the patrols about using better back trail security. I also mentioned to him about taping metal on their gear and not talking while on patrol.

Then I commented that it was no wonder they never found anything. It was like a circus coming to town and they were lucky that someone hadn't set up an ambush for them.

I briefed him on what I had done, and he started laughing. He explained that every man in the firebase had almost jumped out of their skin when the explosions went off. He offered me a cigar, and I took it and lit it. He asked me if I did this often. I told him I never did anything the same way twice.

In the bush you don't ever want to fall into a pattern of movement or activity. If you did, Sir Charles would make things very unpleasant. The Captain walked out of the bunker, but came right back with some hot coffee. I thanked him, and told him that it was not over yet.

I explained in simple and direct terms what we were trying to do to the NVA's thought process. I told him we might have two or three more nights of fun and games. Then I said thanks for the coffee and cigar, and lay down to get some rest. He said he would check back with me later, and walked out.

I woke up a couple of times during the day, and found out that I was the subject of discussion between many of the soldiers in the firebase. I had unofficially been named "The Ghost". That suited me just fine. If my own people weren't able to figure me out, then maybe the NVA wouldn't figure me out either.

That evening I again went out at the back of the patrol, dropped off and started my search. Approximately 2300 I detected movement in the bush moving toward the firebase.

The NVA had returned with another mortar team, but this time they had 4 security people with them. I slowly followed them till they selected a location, and started setting up the tube.

The guards were much closer to the tube this time. In addition, they were set up in pairs, with each member of the pair looking in a different direction.

This was like a game of high stakes poker. I had placed a bet last night, and now my bet had been called, and the ante had been raised. I knew that this was going to have to be handled in a very different way than the action last night.

I moved away from them, changed my AK-47 for my Winchester, and circled around behind them. The mortar team had the tube set up and had just opened a crate containing the mortar rounds.

After some thought, I decided to let them make the mistakes. I was set up in a very dark brushy area. My only clean shot was at the mortar team. I settled in and got my sight picture of the loader. I shot him and his assistant in the head. They both went down with a muffled thump. One of the guards had seen the two VC at the tube collapse.

He and his partner were looking around in every direction trying to figure out where the threat was. After about 10 minutes, they called to the other guard pair, and they all came in together around the tube.

When they had been standing by the tube for about a minute, I started firing at them. I took 3 down immediately, but the forth hit the dirt behind the bodies of the other VC.

I knew he would have to move eventually, so I just kept my eye on the night vision scope and waited. I eventually caught sight of him crawling away toward the brush. When he was almost to the brush, I shot him twice.

I watched for about 30 minutes, but no other activity appeared. I went and pulled the last guard back to the tube and primed two more white phosphorus charges with a timer on each. I dropped one in the tube, and the other in the case of mortar rounds.

Then I quickly but quietly moved away from the area. I had set the timed charge for 15 minutes to make sure I had plenty of time to get well clear of the area. I was about 100 meters away when the explosions lit up the jungle. The firebase immediately shot some flares up and went on full alert again.

By this time I was in deep brush and not moving. I held that position for almost two hours. When no one came to investigate, I slowly moved back toward the camp. I watched the patrol walk up the hill by me and into the firebase.

About 30 minutes after dawn, I threw a red smoke grenade out to get the guard's attention. Then I yelled out that I was coming in. I got up and walked up to the firebase and went directly to the command bunker again.

I cleaned my weapons and washed up. I had heard a chopper land and take off, but I had not gone out of the bunker to see what was going on. After a few minutes, the Captain came in with a hot breakfast. It had come in with the chopper. It was pretty good to eat something that was both warm and reasonably tasty.

The Captain and I talked about the action of last night. I told him that my usefulness was probably at an end, because if the VC came back again, it would be a larger force then I could handle. He agreed and went to call for a chopper to come and get me.

Just after lunch a chopper came in and picked me up. When I got back to Nakhon Phanom I went over to the map room and talked to Mike. He said the Captain had reported to his superior about my actions. The report had already gone up the chain of command and come back down to Mike.

He told me that I was now known as "The Ghost". We had a good laugh then went over to the club for a couple of drinks. It was just another trip **Inside the World of Mirrors**. I flew back out to Korea the next day.

Chapter 6
The Color of Life and Death

This trip was the first time that I had flown directly into Saigon. I now had a new perfume to recognize a country by, and I had a feeling that it would not be worth the price I would pay.

I was met at the airbase by William Parker, the COS at the embassy. We went to MACV and I deposited most of my equipment in a Security area. Then we went to lunch.

The lunch was on the second floor, and the food was superb. It turned out that this was the mess hall for senior officers. We were there because of William's status. He told me in general terms that a briefing would be held at 1400 in the annex behind the main building. I just nodded my head and kept eating.

After lunch we walked over to an area just outside the annex. I thought I was totally crazy. The area was setup with picnic tables. William just laughed at my expression and said the brass like their little comforts. As far as I was concerned, this was just another indication that the people running the war had no idea what was happening in the field.

It was not the first time that this opinion had crossed my mind. One of the servers came along, and gave us both a cold coke. It even had a glass with ice in it. I was now absolutely positive that the people at this facility were totally out of touch with reality. It was no wonder that units in the field felt like they were being put out on a deserted island by themselves.

At 1400 we were sitting in the briefing room in the annex. We were sitting about 3 rows back and to the far left side of the room. I soon understood why.

I had never seen so many general officers in one place in my life. Each one was accompanied by a Captain or a Major. If silver stars could win a war, then we were in the right place and in great shape.

When the chairs in front of us were all filled in, the briefer stood up and went to the podium in the front of the room. He discussed the future intention to have regular army and marine units involved in a full scale invasion of Cambodia.

He noted that this would be a significant historical point in the history of the war because to this point we had not been involved in Cambodia.

I leaned over to William and in a whisper asked if the briefer knew where I had been working. The reply was a negative nod of the head and a shrug of the shoulders.

It was not a surprise that we were struggling to fight the war. The people that were in charge didn't even know or care what we were doing. It was a disgusting thought. I was just not ready for this type of dissimilation. I bit my lip and kept my mouth shut.

The briefer was proposing a training cycle for the advanced teams that would be leading the way into Cambodia. He was proposing that one of the few people that had been in the area set up a training program for the regular troops. It was the first time since the briefing began that something had been said that actually made sense. It then dawned on me that this probably was the reason that I was here. The thought just didn't set well with me.

The briefing was concluded when the Senior Officer told them to put a program into effect immediately. He expected to go into Cambodia sometime in the next 6 or 7 months.

All I could think of was if it was 6 or 7 months away, the NVA and VC would be well informed and ready to meet us. It was a well known fact that the ARVN (Army of South Vietnam) were riddled with informers. When, not if, the ARVN command structure would learn of this mission, then it was sure to be a mess for the American troops when they got there.

We sat still while all the brass walked out, then went up front to the briefer. William told him that I was the man that he had told him about. He then went on to start to tell him about where I had been working and for how long.

I interrupted him and made it very clear that any further discussion of my background or activities would prevent me from participating in this SNAFU (Situation Normal All Fucked Up).

William got upset with me and said I had no say in the matter. I pulled out my 22 berretta from under my shirt, and said I don't think you understand what I just said. He turned and stormed out of the building leaving me with the briefer.

The briefer apologized for what had just happened. It turned out he was an officer from the Army Rangers, and understood my point of view. He then asked if I could help him implement a program of training so that the regular troops would not walk into Cambodia without at least knowing a few basic things.

I asked him where his office was, and he pointed at the main building at MACV. I asked if he had privacy there so that I could speak freely with him. He said he could arrange that when we got to his office. He would let his two enlisted men off for the afternoon. Then we could close the door and talk freely.

I motioned for him to follow me. We went out of the annex and found some picnic tables with nobody close to them. I told him to go and get rid of his men, then to come back and get me. He agreed and walked off. I waved at one of the servers, got another coke with ice, and sat back to wait for his return.

When he came back, I just got up and followed him back into the building. When we got to his office, he closed the door to the hallway and we sat down at a table. I had him explain what he thought the training program was going to teach according to the mission plan that he had been given.

As I suspected, it was written by staff officers to please the generals that would be reading it. The plan as presented was a waste of time. I clearly expressed my opinion and sat back waiting for him to explode.

He surprised me by saying that he was glad that I felt that way, because he agreed with me. He had been brought in from a ranger company in the field to handle this project. He had no idea of how to get the plan changed, as the brass had signed off on it.

I told him that we wouldn't ask the head brass to change their point of view. We would just train 5 or 6 of his best rangers in the real world then report back to the brass that we were making progress in the implementation of a training program.

He asked me how I expected to get away with doing that. I told him they would never know, because they would never leave their ivory tower and wallow in the mud with the rest of us to find out what we were doing. He laughed, and asked me to tell him exactly what I was proposing.

I suggested one day of classroom discussions, followed by a real 3 day patrol. Then take a day off and repeat the process. At the end of this time, his rangers would at least know the basics of working in Cambodia.

I spent several hours explaining the differences that we dealt with in SIO. When we had finished his expression was grim. He had realized that everything they taught at An Khe, the ranger training facility in South Vietnam, would eventually need to be heavily enhanced. All the basic things were currently present, but several very important details were not.

I invited him to be among the first class since he was going to be responsible for the training program. He said that made sense. He suggested that we go to the An Khe ranger training facility and give it a try.

I agreed, and he went out to inform the powers that be that he was going to be gone for a few days while he was getting the program set up. I knew that he was a good officer, because he was more interested in the welfare of his troops than the opinion of the people with silver stars on their shoulders.

When he came back, he said he had made arrangements for us to fly out tomorrow morning. Since I was in Saigon, he would take me out to dinner tonight. We went down to the security room, and I retrieved my 22 berretta with an extra clip of ammunition. Then I had the rest of my gear locked up again.

He took me out that night to a hotel with a restaurant on the roof. It was plush, and full of senior officers, businessmen, and lots of well dressed women. The food was very good, and the view was even better. After dinner we had a drink then returned to the MACV compound.

He had arranged a room for me in the visiting dignitary area. It was as plush as any 4 star-hotel in the U.S. It even had a complimentary wet bar. We talked for a few more minutes, and agreed to meet at the security room at 0900. He left and I pushed a chair up against the door and went to bed.

The next morning we met as agreed, picked up my gear, and immediately jumped in a jeep to go to the chopper pad. By 1100 we were in the air. The flight was only about 60 minutes, and we were on the ground at the in-country ranger training facility.

We secured my equipment and he showed me around. The most interesting thing he showed me was a training area known as "Death Valley". It was the finishing school test for rangers. It was a trail that meandered back and forth across a small stream, and was full of booby traps and other games that the VC liked to play.

No one had ever walked the course without setting off one of the devices or stepping on something he should have known about. He suggested I try the course in the morning and see what their last training test was like.

I looked at him for a moment and said "What's wrong with Now"? He just blinked a couple of times, and went over to make arrangements with the NCOs in charge. I told him that I would take about an hour to get ready. We went back to security, picked up my gear, and went to the room in the BOQ (Bachelor's Officers Quarters) that had been arranged for me.

I changed my clothes and got my gear together. When I came out he was surprised. I was not wearing a U.S. standard field uniform. I was wearing a variation of the French Splinter pattern that the NVA used. In addition, my boots had rubber tire tread just like most of the NVA wore.

I answered his question before he could ask it. I'm wearing this because if someone sees me at a distance, they will think that I am one of their soldiers. If they saw my tracks somewhere, they would just assume it was one of their own people.

I then pulled an AK-47 out of my bag and said they couldn't tell where the enemy was if it sounded just like their weapons. I put on my camouflage, and put a bandanna over my hair. It was time to go find out what new things I could learn.

When we returned to "Death Valley" the NCOs were ready for

me. I could tell by their grins that they had made every effort to make sure I failed the course. I was given the standard briefing, and told where I was to go.

I sat down on the ground and checked all my equipment. Everything was taped down and in order. I went to the sign that said "Start here" and began to move.

They had rushed a little when they added the extra tricks, because it was easy to see where they had been set up. In most cases at least a few of the leaves were turned the wrong way so they would show up as a lighter color. I also never went near the path. I started out down the 2 kilometer course by moving well uphill and away from the path. Three hours later I crossed the finish line.

The smirks on the NCOs were gone. I found out later that the course had over 80 traps scattered between the start and the finish and that no trainee had ever walked the course without setting off one of the traps.

Each trap was setup with a smoke grenade to show the trainee that he had been killed. I had not set off one of the traps. One NCO complained that I had not really walked the course. I said congratulations; you've just learned the first rule of working in Cambodia. You should never go anywhere near a trail. In addition, you never move more than 10 or 15 feet before you stop and check out the area.

I explained the camouflage problems with the leaves not being set up the correct way. I had never put my foot down on any covered surface. I continued my explanation for about 10 more minutes. Then I offered to join them at the NCO clubs for a few drinks on me.

I went back to my room, cleaned up, and went to the NCO club. There had been 4 ranger NCOs at the "Death Valley" course, and they were waiting at the club for me to arrive. But the size of the group had grown to about 15 NCOs. They all wanted to see the first man who had walked "Death Valley" successfully.

I bought all the NCO's a drink, and after a while we had reached a level of grudging respect. I suggested that the trainers at the "Death Valley" course be the first people to go through the new field training. Since they were already used to training activities, I suggested that they would be the best people to add the things that they learned to their current training program. They all agreed subject to approval by the Captain.

The Captain approved each of the 4 NCOs to go through the process with me. He surprised me when he said he wanted to be involved also. Maybe my first observation of him was correct. We would find out starting in the morning.

We started the next morning, and had discussions till late in the afternoon. The NCOs had realized that what I was doing wasn't all that different from what they were used to doing. I was aware that, to them, it would seem like they were only minor details. I had to push them to understand that the differences in Cambodia would help keep them alive. The differences may have seemed subtle, but the end result would be very different. They had now begun to realize how slow and careful they had to be.

I'm not sure they totally believed me when I told them about the NVA and VC concentrations across the border. They would soon learn that I wasn't exaggerating. We set up a departure time of 1300 hours for tomorrow. We would meet at 1100 hours and go over the check list I lived by.

They showed up the next morning at the appointed time, and were embarrassed when I found at least one or two things wrong with the way they were dressed and prepared for the mission.

We spent the next hour correcting each small but vital point and discussing why it was important. We walked to the chopper pad and took off.

They were surprised when the chopper teams did 2 fake insertions before they dropped us off at a cold LZ about 2 kilometers from Cambodia. As we all huddled together in the brush, I told them the chopper crew would do at least one or two more fake insertions to keep the NVA and VC guessing what was going on.

I picked the most junior NCO and had him lead off as point man. I changed the point man about every 300 meters, so I could get a feeling for each of their skill levels and attention to detail. When they had all had a turn on point, I showed them how to loop around to check if we were being followed.

Then I had us practice setting up a RON (Rest-Over-Night) site. I taught them about the string communication method and the wheel formation with all our feet in the middle and everyone pointed out. By the time we were set up properly, it was dark. I set up the watch schedule, and handed the first man a night vision scope. Then we turned in for the night.

The next morning, we broke camp and headed out again. This time we were actually going into Cambodia. I was walking slack as the second man in the line so that I could watch what the point man was doing.

We came over the top of a hill, staying in deep brush, when I called a halt. I told the rest of the team behind me to stay where they were. I then crawled up to where the point man was kneeling.

I asked if he saw the enemy positions. He blinked his eyes, looked around again, and shook his head no. I told him to look across the valley below us to the upslope on the next hill.

He still didn't see the enemy positions. I finally pointed them out. They had been a little careless about the camouflage on their positions. There were areas where the color of the vegetation was lighter that the other areas around it.

I explained that this was probably a two or three man position, and that they had either not made sure the top of the leaf surface was facing out, or they had let the camouflage vegetation get too dry. Either way, it was not a natural occurrence in nature, so it had to be manmade.

The only people in this area that would do this were the enemy troops. When we were finished, he had eventually found 7 potential problem sites. I showed him two more sites that he had missed. I told him that what he was seeing was the "Color of Life and Death". See it and live or miss it and die.

I had him crawl back to the team and send up the next man. I warned him not to explain to any of them what they were looking for. He nodded his head, and crawled away. I repeated this with each member of the team. They were a little ashamed that they had not seen it.

I had us all pull back over the hill and circle up to an area of dense brush. I waited for about 30 minutes, then I went to each one individually, stressing that this was just the tip of iceberg. Now they knew something new to look for. It wasn't their fault that no one had ever showed this to them. I commended their professional attitude and the skill levels that they had been demonstrating.

I had the man on the radio call in an air strike on the hill where the VC was hiding. We specifically requested Napalm be used. We gave them the map coordinates, and then backed off about 300 meters further away into deep brush.

About 40 minutes later the Air Force contacted us on the radio. We made sure they had the right aiming point, and we sat back to watch. It was a four plane flight, with two making a north to south run about 2 minutes before the other two planes followed them in. The first pass only hit about 3 of the sites, so I got on the radio and had them move their drop zone about 50 meters further up the hill. This time it was a perfect drop. I looked at the rest of the team, and said. "See what a difference color makes!"

This process continued as we moved around for another two days. When we called in the chopper for extraction, and I taught them about circling the LZ with a silenced weapon, we went back to their home. It wasn't my home. I no longer had a home.

I hadn't told them the story of what I was becoming or how I had been christened the "Ghost", or how maybe I was starting to be one. Someday the transition would be complete, or maybe not.

The Captain sent us all to get cleaned up, and we were to meet at 1500 hours at the classroom in the main building. I took my time getting over to the meeting. I walked in about 5 minutes late.

I was now dressed in my night mission uniform. The uniform was completely black. I had black camouflaged coloring on my face, neck, and arms. I was carrying my AK-47, my 22 caliber Winchester with the night site mounted, and had my 22 berretta with silencer hung on my pistol belt. Thus began a new set of lessons.

We reviewed what we had learned up to this point. The Captain was especially pleased with how we were progressing. The senior NCO asked me how I had learned all these details.

I surprised them when I told them about my initial jungle training in Panama. I told them that I had been taught almost every single thing I knew from the 4 Rangers that worked with me in Panama. But the real details had been bought and paid for by the deaths of many fine men that I had worked real missions with.

I stressed that a silenced weapon was almost always a necessity. I let them handle each of my weapons. The captain said he didn't know where to get the gear and weapons that I had taught them about. I just handed him a phone number and told him to use my name. He went off to make the call.

I answered some general questions then we broke up and set a meeting time at the NCO club of 2000. I walked out and went to my quarters to clean up.

We had the next day off, so we stayed a little late. The Captain came in and bought a round of drinks for the men. A few minutes later he pulled me to the side, and said that the gear would be delivered in the morning. Each man would have his choice of silenced weapons.

I nodded and waited for him to continue. He was just a little too tense for the surroundings at the club. I was sure that he had something else to say.

When we broke, he asked me to join him in his room for a few minutes. He was trying to be casual, but still showed the tension I had noticed earlier. We walked down the street and into the BOQ.

When we sat down in his room, he told me that a mission order had arrived while we were out in the field. MACV was getting in the way again.

The mission orders were for an in-depth survey of enemy positions and strength. Some idiot at MACV had sold this idea to the brass. What they were asking for may have seemed reasonable to the brass, but to me it was an invitation to disaster. I was once again being sent into the dragon's lair with poorly prepared soldiers. It was another invitation to disaster.

The detail that MACV was asking for was simply not possible to get and still stay alive. We talked for a little while longer then I left and went to my room. Things had just turned ugly, and I was being told to count the scales on the back of the dragon without his knowing that I had been there.

I didn't sleep well, and as a result, was not in the best of moods the next morning. We met at the classroom after breakfast. This time the Major in command of the Ranger Company was sitting at the table in the front of the room.

The rest of the people I had worked with were seated and waiting for me to arrive. The Captain introduced the Major, and we sat down to talk. I listened to what was being discussed without saying a word. Finally, the Major looked at me and asked what I was thinking.

I told him that I was not in favor of the mission. The odds of success were minimal and the mission as planned was a good way to kill some really fine soldiers.

It took him a while to realize that I was absolutely serious. I could give him a pretty good idea of what we faced from my previous experiences. The area was known to be riddled with tunnels. Somewhere in the maze a hospital and about 3000 or 4000 NVA were waiting for us to be crazy enough to come and visit. He had a scowl on his face when I was done.

The Major began to talk about the mission requirements, and that he had no choice but to try to get the results they wanted. He clearly understood that he would be replaced if he didn't run the missions. They would simply send someone else to take command and issue the orders. It was totally unfair to the Major because it would effectively end his military career advancement.

He was being squeezed from MACV, and was decidedly unhappy about it. I suggested that we take a ten minute break, and with the approval of the Major, I went outside to walk and think. Along the way I bummed a cigarette off of one of the NCOs.

I could see it happening all over again. People were being sent to do something that they had almost no information about with only minimal training and experience for this job. This type of thinking by the brass upstairs was directly responsible for a large portion of the casualties the American forces were taking. I have no idea how to explain this process more clearly except to emphasize the damage that it had caused.

I walked around a little longer than I planned to, but soon gave up thinking about it and went back to the classroom. I apologized to the Major for being late, and tried to explain my feelings and concerns. He never interrupted while I was talking. He just looked me straight in the eye and listened.

When I finally ran down, he said he appreciated the concern that I had for his personnel, but that the situation was unchanged. They were going to start patrolling across the border. He would do everything that he could to help us, but his hands were tied. I could tell that he wasn't happy about the mission parameters or the corner in which he was trapped.

He asked me what could actually be done to achieve at least some of what he was being told to do. We all talked for over an hour, but still hadn't come up with anything substantial.

I finally suggested that we use an approach that I had seen used in the past. We would go in as a small 3 man team. Our movement would be slow, but would be aided by a set of diversionary explosions that would pull the NVA away from us and toward the noise.

The Air Force would have to drop some bombs about 4 kilometers away from our patrol pattern. The helicopter gunships would then begin to strike the bombed area as if they were prepping a large LZ for a sizeable insertion of troops.

My suggestion was based on the same idea a matador uses with the bull he is facing. It was all about misdirection, and giving the enemy a pattern that they would recognize and react to in a predictable manner.

I also said that whatever we found out, it could be embellished by our experiences. We wouldn't lie to the brass. We would just not tell them everything we were going to do. The Major looked at me for a moment or two then asked if I really thought we could get away with it. My reply was direct and simple. I saw no other way to approach the problem. He just stared at me.

The Captain asked the Major to let us work on a plan. We would have something for him by tomorrow evening. The Major looked around the room at the team members, nodded his head, and walked out. We were now on our own. He had given the orders as he was required to do.

We just wouldn't tell him any specific details so that he wouldn't have to lie when he reported back to the brass at MACV.

I told the Captain that he was not going on the mission. He would have the same problem as the major if he knew what was happening. He didn't like it, but knew I was right. He shook hands with each of the rangers sitting at the table, thanked me, and walked out.

I then explained who I wanted to go with me on the mission. The senior NCO and the junior NCO were both good soldiers, but I felt that the other two NCOs had picked up on what I was trying to show them a little more quickly. In addition, both were slender and wiry. When it came time to run, which I was sure would eventually happen, the wiry guys could probably go longer and further than the others.

The two NCOs I had picked were both several years older than I was, but they didn't know that. It was just assumed that I was in charge. With the selection process complete the two NCOs who were not picked shook hands with us and left the room.

We spent the next two hours getting all the details of the plan together. We broke up, and I told the NCOs that I would meet them at the club in about 30 minutes with a reminder not to breathe a word about what we were trying to put together.

I walked over to the BOQ and spoke to the Captain. He had to get in touch with the Air Force and helicopter gunships to be sure that they had a slot open to be our diversion. When we went in depended on when they were able to schedule the diversionary attack.

At the club that night, I only had one drink. My mind was buzzing. I finally gave up, and told the two NCOs to meet me at the classroom at 1100 hours and went to the BOQ to get some sleep.

I really did not like how dependent we were on so many different moving parts. I drifted off to sleep thinking that we would find out tomorrow whether or not this crazy scheme would really happen.

After breakfast the next morning, I checked in with the Captain. He had the ball rolling, but had no answers back yet. He expected to know before the day was over. I thanked him and walked over toward the classroom.

I leaned against the side of a bunker and lit a cigarette. I would have to work hard not to let my concerns mess up the two NCOs that I was going with. I was always anxious before every mission, but this one seemed to make me worry a lot more than usual.

We met as agreed at the classroom, and went over the plan several times. We were trying to figure out where something could go wrong, and how we would deal with it. If we became separated, we established a fall back meeting point. Then we went to lunch.

While we were eating, the Captain came in and put an envelope on the table beside me. We chatted for a couple of minutes for appearance sake, and he left. I put my arm down on the envelope and slid it back off the table onto my lap. As we continued to talk, I pushed the envelope inside my shirt.

We then left and went down to the Armory. The new silenced equipment had arrived, and I helped each NCO pick the silenced weapon that he was going to take. We walked out to the range, and they practiced putting the weapons together and taking them apart. Since both were using silence pistols, it only took a few minutes before they were comfortable with the weapons.

Upon arrival back at the classroom, we discovered a regularly scheduled class in session. I suggested that we go back to my room and make our final plans.

Once we were in my room I pulled out the envelope. The Air Force had gotten involved in a big way. Someone had decided that this was a chance to get some serious practice in. They had two flights of four jets that would strike the area that we had requested at 1700 hours two days from now. The gunships were scheduled to play their game at 1830 hours.

That put us on the ground just before dark tomorrow to work our way to a position to start the patrol. We would hit the ground at 1600 hours and move toward the patrol area. We would wait over night and all day for the show to begin.

I set 1200 as the time for us to get together and make sure we had everything we needed and were ready to go. They went off to get some sleep, and I sat on the bed and stared at the wall. I finally gave up and lay down to try to sleep.

We all got together at 1200. They were properly set up for the bush. Everything was taped down and blacked out. The canteens were full so that we would not slosh when we moved. I gave each one of them a pair of night vision goggles. They would show a green ghostly picture of the terrain, and would pick up on the extra heat that would be coming out of tunnel entrances or any half hidden enemy soldiers.

The chopper picked us up on schedule and we went off to the LZ. I had my AK-47, my Winchester with both scopes and the silencer, and my 22 berretta with its silencer. They also had AK-47s. We each had 300 rounds of ammunition for the AK-47s, and about 50 rounds for each silenced weapon. We all carried Chinese grenades.

Fifteen minutes out we got the high sign from the crew chief. At 5 minutes we were standing on the skids. The helicopter never landed. It just hovered about 3 feet off the ground, and we jumped out and headed for the nearest pile of brush.

The chopper was gone before we had all made it to the bushes. I gave the hand signal for silenced weapons, and put the AK-47 slung over my shoulder and took my Winchester with the night scope in my hands.

We stayed where we were for about 10 minutes. We had detected no movement around us, so we moved out. At 2030 I signaled for a loop back and movement into dense brush to check our tail. It was an automatic action for me. I still did it even though I had never found anyone behind me. That changed almost immediately.

Shortly after we had looped back to check our tail, two NVA soldiers came down the hill we had just negotiated. They were not near the trail, and were moving very close to the path we had taken coming down the hill.

I signaled that I would take the shots. I waited until the NVA were almost even with us when I took aim at the soldier in back. I took him down with one shot, and his partner was turning around to see what had cause the noise that was made when he took two rounds and went down on the ground. I put another round into the one that had been shot first.

We did not move immediately. After five minutes I felt reasonably sure that they were by themselves. I gave my Winchester to one of the NCOs, pulled out my 22 berretta, and took the other NCO with me. We went to the NVA and picked them up. We carried them about 30 meters further into the heavy brush and dumped them.

I sent the NCO with me back to where the other NCO was in overwatch. He signaled to me that it still looked clear, so I went back down to the place where we had picked them up. There were blood stains on the ground. I picked up dirt and leaves and covered the blood stains as best I could. Maybe the next people coming along would not walk through that area and see anything suspicious.

After returning to the two NCOs, I signaled that we were going to move to our RON. I took the lead, and we set off. We had traveled about a kilometer when we heard faint talking. We couldn't understand what was being said, or even what language it was in. We just knew that it was a human voice.

We moved into very heavy brush, and watched as the NVA patrol came walking by. They were about 50 meters away from us and following the trail. They were very casual. They had done this many times, and never found anything. They passed by without seeing us.

I pulled the team tightly together and whispered that the casual manner the patrol had demonstrated was the first good news of the night. I stressed again to be careful about noise, and we set off again.

About 0300 we found a really good hide location, and did a loop back to check our tail. After 10 minutes no one had appeared and we quietly moved into the hide. I designated watch order, and we connected ourselves by string. I took the first watch, and the NCOs lay down on their stomachs and went to sleep.

The night passed with no further action. As we rotated through the watch routine, I made sure that each NCO would use the Night Vision goggles only if they heard or thought they saw something. If you use them too much, your night vision would be get completely shot.

We stayed where we were all day. We heard a patrol pass by us on the trail down the hill, but they were very casual like the first patrol. At 1700 hours we heard the first explosions from the Air Force bombing runs. This continued for about 15 minutes. We packed up, and got ready to move. At 1820, just a little early, we heard the gunships begin their show. They kept at it for about 10 minutes then left the area.

We still did not move. I was waiting for a patrol to come running by us heading toward the location where all the noise had come from. About 10 minutes later, we heard them coming. There were about 10 members of the patrol, moving at a fast pace toward the area that had been bombed and strafed. As soon as they were out of sight, we moved out in the direction that they had come from.

It was apparent that the bombing and strafing had done the job. Twice in the next 40 minutes we had to go to ground to avoid other groups of NVA running toward the site of the diversion attack.

I had one of the NCOs looking through a single lens night vision scope. He wasn't looking for any NVA troops. He was looking for what would look like a small white geyser or cloud of fog. He slipped up beside me and told me where to look. I took the scope. He had found a tunnel entrance. The warmth in the tunnels would show up on the night vision scope like water spewing up out of a fountain if the tunnel was open. If it was closed, it would look like a soft cloud of fog. He took a moment to mark the place on one of our maps and we moved on.

In the next hour we found 5 more tunnel entrances. We had only traveled about 1 kilometer. I figured we must be right on top of the main tunnel complex.

I turned us around and headed back up the hill staying in heavy brush. Just before we got to the top of the hill, I stopped and checked out the tall mountain ridge about 400 meters away. I scanned the area with the night vision scope, and found a number of softly glowing areas almost at the top of the ridge.

These were obviously camouflaged positions. From the location along the top of the ridge, I figured that these were anti-aircraft sites. We took the map and marked them down.

We were still in the deep brush when we heard what sounded like a tank. I knew we didn't have any armor in the area, so whatever it was belonged to the bad guys. We held our position for about 20 minutes more when the NCO next to me pulled at my sleeve and pointed across the valley to a trail coming down the side of the hill.

I was so surprised that I almost spoke out loud. It certainly looked like a little tank. Later, after reflecting on the incident, I realized that it was an old Soviet T-34 tank. I marked it on the map. It was now about 0200. It was necessary to get out of the immediate area and into a solid hide. Daylight was only a few hours away.

We moved on over the hill and started down the other side. It was suddenly very quiet. No sounds of birds were in the air. With all the noise that had occurred earlier, I expected that the animals in the area would be making all sorts of noise. Even the monkeys were absolutely quiet.

I froze and signaled for the team to hit the dirt. We went down and behind some bushes. The hair was standing up on the back of my neck. Every alarm was going off in my brain, but I hadn't figured out why. After a couple of minutes it suddenly occurred to me that the animals would be noisy as you passed through an area, but if you had a large group and stayed near where the animals were, they would become quiet.

I used the ambush hand signal to get my team's attention. After another 10 minutes, I motioned for the last NCO in line to crawl back over the hill top. When he was over the top, I sent the other NCO after him. I had my night scope on my Winchester and was scanning back and forth across the hill on the other side of the valley.

I caught a soldier changing from one position to another. I had been right. We had almost walked into an ambush that would surely have killed all three of us.

I started crawling back up and went over the hill. I pulled my team in close and explained what I had seen and what it meant. We were in deep trouble. The enemy had responded to the diversion in such a way as to let us into the area without much problem. But that was hours ago, and now they had troops out in ambush positions looking for any patrol or individual movement.

We couldn't go back the way we came, and didn't know what we might find in another direction. If we found anything, it was bound to be more trouble, especially if they saw us first.

We worked our way about 400 meters north of the ambush position, and found a great hide. Three sides of it were what we called "tangle-foot vines". If you tried to move through it, you would get so tangled up that you would literally have to be cut out the vines by your teammates. The other side had two large stands thorn bushes. We went in on our stomachs, and still got scratched with every move.

When we were finally all inside the thorn bushes, we cut down some tangle-foot vines and spread them along the sides of the thorn bushes. We backed into the hole we had cut out of the tangle-foot vines.

We were not going to move till tomorrow night unless something bad happened. The only way someone could see us was to climb through the thorn bushes.

In whispers, I explained that we were not moving till it was dark again. We were not going to move even to take a piss. It might not be pleasant, but you would stay alive that way. None of us got much rest during the day. Several times large patrols walked within 20 meters of our location, and never thought about looking inside to see if anyone was there.

The two NCOs were scared and shaky. That made them one step better off than me, because I knew what our chances were tonight when we tried to get out. They were still thinking that if no one found us during the day, then we could move out that night.

About 1600 hours I heard the tank go by and back up the hill. Soon after that a bugle sounded. Within 30 minutes two patrols walked right by us going down the hill. By 1900, it was pitch dark and starting to rain. While that made the conditions miserable, it also made it easier for us to move quietly when we took off.

I woke up the team, and in whispers, explained what we were going to do. Fifteen minutes later I was out of the brush with my Winchester in my hands and was scanning the area through the night scope. It took about 5 minutes for the rest of the team to crawl out through the thorn bushes.

We immediately went north away from the tunnel complex staying about 10 meters under the crest of the hill. When we reached areas where the brush was thin, we crawled. This went on for over 3 hours.

I hadn't seen a sign of the NVA ambushes I was worried about. I hadn't even seen a patrol. They were out there somewhere, I just didn't know where. I pulled us into some dense brush, and we took a break. Moving like we were moving was a terrible strain on the body and the nerves. I let us rest until 0130, when we moved out again.

I stayed on point more than I let the NCOs do it. It was not that I was better at moving than they were. I had stayed alive this long by paying attention to my feelings and hunches. I had decided to find a hide and pull up for another day when the NCO with the night vision scope saw a glow. It was small, but it was definitely there.

It wasn't big enough to be a patrol or a multiple man site. I decided that it was either the biggest monkey in Cambodia or it was a trail watcher. I was pretty sure it was the latter. We moved to within 100 meters of his position when I signaled the team to wait while I handled the trail watcher. I left them the night vision scope and told them when they saw the trail watcher go down, to come up and join me.

It is tough to stalk a sentry in the light bush, but with enough discipline and attention to detail it can be done. I really didn't have to get real close. I figured 20 or 30 meters with a good clean shot angle would be close enough.

Just as I was about to shoot the sentry, another man came walking down the trail. This was obviously an NCO checking the sentry positions along the trail. That meant that more sentry positions would have to be found and worked around.

I don't know why, but I suddenly decided it was a good idea to shoot both of them. I had a great sight picture in the scope. I put two rounds in the NCO, then two rounds in the sentry. I stood up and waved the team to come forward.

We grabbed the bodies and hauled them about 20 meters up the hill and left them behind some thick bushes. Now we had no choice. We had to move and clear the area. I didn't know when, but someone would come looking for the NCO or the sentry.

It started raining again, and that made it much easier to move through the bush. By 0400 we had moved about 3 kilometers and had found another good hide. We were well away from any trail, and we needed to shut down for the day. We looped around to check our tail, and when nothing appeared, we moved into the hide. We spent the day quietly. We needed the rest. We were almost out of food, and the last of the water that we had we picked up when we crossed a small stream.

During the day I had been able to see enough of the area around us to have our position figured out. I estimated that we were only 2 or 3 kilometers away from our primary extraction LZ. We were almost exactly on the border of Cambodia and South Vietnam.

We were close enough to our LZ to be able to reach the FAC. We got on the radio and called the FAC. He responded on our second try. We set up a pickup at 2400. This would be a quick hover and go for the chopper. We would have the site secured and be ready to jump on board.

We moved out slowly at 1930. It would rain for 30 minutes then stop for a little while. The weather was on-again off-again all the way to the LZ. That was just the break we needed. We reached the area around the LZ at 2300. I went around the LZ, followed by the NCOs, and found no enemy around the site.

We stayed in deep brush till the FAC called us and told us the chopper was 5 minutes out. I acknowledged and we moved up to the edge of the clearing and turned on an infrared beacon.

The chopper came over the trees on the other side of the LZ and dropped down so fast I thought he was going to crash. The pilot really knew what he was doing. The chopper touched down with hardly a bump. We ran out and jumped on the Huey, and they took off.

We were all totally spent. It wasn't the physical activity; it was the tension and mental strain that had us drained. We all three went to sleep on the way back. The crew chief woke us up when we are about ten minutes out.

There was a truck waiting for us when the chopper landed. We were taken to the Ranger compound and dropped at the TOC.

The Major and the Captain were standing in the door waiting to greet us. I sent the two NCOs to the armory to secure our gear, and went over to talk to the two Ranger leaders. I just told them that it was a tough row to hoe, but we had got it done. I bummed a cigarette and sat down on the sandbag by the door to the TOC.

I asked the officers to be patient for just a few more minutes. I wanted to have the other two NCOs back with me when we debriefed and gave our reports.

An NCO inside the TOC came out and handed me a cup of coffee. I nodded my thanks and told him we would need two more for the NCOs that were coming back.

When the NCOs returned, I let them handle the majority of the debriefing. They made it abundantly clear that it was the toughest area they had ever been in. When we gave them the positions of the probable anti-aircraft sites they were really surprised.

By the time we gave them the locations of the tunnel entrances, and told them about the tank, they were shaking their heads. At the end of the debriefing I joking asked if all the scratches from the thorn bushes would qualify us for a purple heart.

Two days later I flew to Saigon, then on to Japan and Korea. Once more into the breach I had gone and come back again. It was just another trip **Inside the World of Mirrors**.

I felt sorry for the main body of troops that would be going in to Cambodia. A lot of people would die because of poor training, or in many cases, no training for the job they were sent to do. It was a common problem that I saw over and over again.

Chapter 7
Who Let the Bureaucrats Run the War

It was almost like a high school homecoming date with a girl who got sick and couldn't go with you to the prom. I was back at Nakhon Phanom to run another mission. This time Mike Simmons wasn't there. He was back in the U.S. for whatever reason, and his temporary replacement was Glenn Parker.

I had never met Glenn before, so I approached our first meeting with trepidation. I had no idea how much this guy knew, or how much his job was going to go to his head. I was correct to be worried, because the first words out of his mouth were, "You are going into North Vietnam on a bridge Demolition tomorrow and everything is ready to go"!

This statement blindsided me because Mike Simmons always told me the point of the mission, and then we would go at it back and forth until I was comfortable enough to run the mission. Glenn was making it very clear that he was running this mission, and that I was just a tool he was using to accomplish a purpose.

I took a moment to compose myself before I responded to Glenn. After lighting up a cigarette, I told him he had no say in how I would run a mission. He could tell me the objectives, but not the how and when.

He took it like the bureaucrat that he was. He puffed up and told me that he was the boss. If I didn't like it, then he would just report upstairs that I was not cooperative and thought that I knew all the answers.

I didn't blast him like I could have. I just motioned to the communications center and said let's call the shop and get this cleared up. He told me that he was making no such call. I pulled my berretta out of my pocket and stuck it in his face while telling him that I was going to make the call with or without him. It was his choice. He was red faced with anger, and guaranteed me that I was about to get in over my head in trouble.

I raised my berretta and put a shot in the ceiling above his head while telling him that he had received his last warning. I was serious in everything I said and did. No paper pusher was going to send me out to get killed on just his say so. He went from red faced to very pale.

I stood up and motioned him to the communication room. After a few seconds, he got up and started walking into the room to initiate direct contact with the shop. The whole time he was walking he was ranting and raving about having me put away for about 20 years. My reply was that we would see who got to call the action.

Ten minutes later we were on the line with Woody Woodford back at the shop. I let him tell Woody his side of the situation first. As I expected he stretched his story completely out of proportion.

At the end of his tirade against me, Woody told him to put me on the line. I calmly told Woody exactly what had happened, and that I was not going to run any mission the way he decided I should. I was not about to let some "Pretty Boy" help me commit suicide.

Woody told me to give the phone back to Glenn. Glenn picked up the phone and sat very still as a long one-sided conversation rolled over him. The longer he sat there listening to Woody, the madder he got. He finally slammed down the phone and stalked out of the room.

The communications technician reestablished contact with the shop and Woody immediately came on line. He told me to get the mission requirements from Glenn, and to determine how it could be done. Once that was finished I was to call him back and we would talk again.

For whatever reason, when I went into Glenn's office he would not even acknowledge my presence. He never looked at me even when I spoke to him. My request for the mission specifications was made in a quiet and low level monotone. He ignored me for about 30 seconds, then picked up a folder and threw it at me. The contents scattered all over the floor between us. Glenn then stalked out of the office.

I stared at the empty door he had just left through wondering what the idiot thought he was doing. While picking up the papers and maps, the communications technician came in and told me that it would be normal business hours at the shop in about 12 hours. He suggested that we contact the shop again at that time. I then realized that he had listened to both sides of the conversations with Woody. He knew that I had got Woody out of bed, and was just suggesting that we let him get some rest before we called him back. It was a reasonable suggestion, so I agreed to his schedule.

I sat down at Glenn's desk and started to reorganize the mission maps and information. It took almost 30 minutes to finally get it in usable order. I went to security and had them lock it up for me along with the rest of my gear. Then I went over to the club to get a drink. I knew that if I started working on the mission profile and documentation immediately I would not be able to get Glenn out of my mind and do a realistic mission assessment and plan.

Two drinks and an hour later I was back at security picking up the folder. I went over to an empty team briefing room and started going through the package.

It didn't take long to see that some analyst on the intelligence side of the business was taking a flyer at getting his idea turned into a mission. I had to admit that the idea wasn't totally out in left field, but the actions necessary to make it happen were very stupid.

The mission called for going into North Vietnam and blowing up a train bridge used for the delivery of PRC equipment and supplies. The problem was where the railroad left China and entered into North Vietnam. It was in the northern most portion of North Vietnam and was located about midway between Cao Bang and Lang Son and 30 kilometers inside of North Vietnam.

The actual distance between the bridge and the nearest access point was well over 100 miles in from the South China Sea. There was no way to stage a mission that far into North Vietnam and China border. After about 3 hours, I gave up on the mission. I went to the communications technician and set up a time for the call to the shop.

I let him know what room I was in, and when to send somebody to get me.

Then I went to the chow hall and ate a hot meal. At least it wasn't field rations, so that was a plus. Then it was off to my room until the runner came to get me.

I never really got into a sound sleep. This whole situation was so absurd and ridiculous that my mind wouldn't quit working. I finally got up and went out to sit on the front steps and enjoy the relative quiet of the night. About two hours later the runner came to get me and took me back to the communications room.

Twenty minutes later I was on line with Woody. I explained what I had seen, and stressed how impossible that mission would be. Woody told me to forget about it, and not to bother Glenn. He had another mission profile he wanted me to look at. The package was in the air and would arrive in about 36 hours.

That meant that I had two days to kill, and I wasn't going to spend it in Northern Cambodia. I went to the Air America shop to see if there was anything going to anywhere that I might want to go. There was a flight to Osaka, Japan that would leave in about 2 hours, and would return after a 24 hour layover. I talked my way onto the flight, and went off to enjoy myself. It proved to be a memorable trip that really calmed me down. I was ready to go back to work when we returned.

When I returned to Nakhon Phanom, Woody's package was waiting for me. I had been in and out of the control center and the TOC and hadn't seen Glenn. I quietly asked the communication technician if he knew where Glenn was. He said Glenn had taken a plane to Guam yesterday, and was not expected back.

It looked like the shop had realized that Glenn was an idiot, and got him out of the way before I blew my top and shot or killed him. I figured that it was fine with me that I didn't have to avoid him since he was gone. Mike had not yet returned, so I went into his office and opened the package.

This was a more normal mission, if normal is a word that could be applied in the context of a SIO mission. They wanted a snatch job run in eastern Cambodia. They wanted to get an NCO or Officer that was with any unit going south on the trail.

A snatch job was a mission where you went in, captured someone, and brought them back to Nakhon Phanom. Snatch jobs were difficult because you had to bring the captured person back alive. It was reasonable to assume that such an individual would not be overly cooperative in our endeavor.

I figured it would take a Yard to walk point, three experienced SIO personnel, and a medic to do the job. The Yard was to get us in and out without being seen. The SIO personnel were basically there to carry the prisoner, and the medic was there to keep him doped up enough not to cause us a problem. We would take a stretcher to carry him.

The infiltration and exfiltration points would have to be very close to the area where the mission was running. There was no way we could carry a man on a stretcher through the jungle for any distance without being seen.

This meant we would have to find an area of the trail where we could get in and out quickly. The SIO personnel would need to be strong and in the best condition. They would be running while carrying a stretcher.

After a while, I went back to the communications technician and asked who was in camp that could run a quick mission. He sent me over to see the NCO of a marine recon squad that had been back in from the field for about 3 days.

We discussed the potential mission in detail. The NCO didn't like the long carry with a stretcher. Instead he suggested a modified extraction of the captured soldier by tying him to a penetrator and letting him drag through the air all the way back to the base. I loved the idea. We would be able to move on to another LZ and get our ride home from there much sooner.

He had just run an observation patrol along the trail about 40 kilometers south of Laos inside of Cambodia. It was constantly busy on the trail in that area because it was a major overnight rest stop for the units coming down the trail. It would be almost impossible to get an NCO or Officer because they were in the center of the rest area. To stay overnight, they used a formation like a large circle. The lower the rank, the further they were toward the outside of the circle.

I inquired about a NCO that would be checking the guards but was told that the guards were all within visual distance of the guard on either side of them. If anyone was out of sight for more than a minute or two, the guards would sound the alarm. If this happened, then everyone in the camp would be after us as soon as they put on their boots.

One of the corporals in the recon squad made a good suggestion. He said what if we took down one or two guards with poisoned darts from the Yard, and then put someone in a matching uniform immediately in his place? If we did this to two guards next to each other, then we could shoot the NCO checking the guards with a knockout dart while he was between our two guard impersonators.

A quick check found that there were four other Yards in camp. We could dress both of them up as regular NVA personnel and make it happen pretty quickly. The two Yards would have to stay behind for about 15 minutes to give us time to get away from the snatch point. Then they could just step behind a tree, take off the uniform, and sneak away to join us after we had sent the captured NCO off on the penetrator extraction.

These guys really thought that it would work. I was leery because we had to do far too many things exactly right to make the mission a success. The marine NCO and I walked over to the aviation group to discuss the double pickup program. I guess that enthusiasm really is contagious because they thought that it would work, too.

We set up our infiltration for 0400 in two days. Then we all went off to the club for a few drinks. I slipped out of the club before the rest of the group to write up a mission plan description to be sent to Woody at the office. Then I went off to bed. The next morning after chow, I went back to the communications room to see if Woody had responded.

I had a message waiting for me. The mission was authorized. We would go in tomorrow morning early. I went to the marines and gave them the news. These crazy nuts still thought the mission was a good idea and that it would work. We all sat down and went over the mission plan with special attention to all the small details. The NCO would translate to the Yards and get their agreement on each phase. We ate chow early, and went to bed.

We were at the chopper pad at 0345 and were immediately up and on our way. We hit the LZ two hours later. It was 5 kilometers from the trail area where we were going to be working. It would probably take two nights to get to the area and set up shop. On the way in, we would have to find a location for the penetrator extraction of our prisoner. We moved out and covered about 3 kilometers when we found a good area to hide in. We looped around to check if we were being followed, and when it was apparent that our trail was clean, we moved into the hide.

We set up a watch rotation, and spent the day sleeping and getting ready for the next night's actions. We had found a good area nearby for the penetrator extraction, and called the FAC to give him the coordinates. We would call in when we were ready to do the snatch, and the helicopters would get up in the air to come to us.

At 1900 we loaded up and moved out toward the target area. It was a slow process to close in on a known enemy concentration of personnel and not be seen or heard. By 0215 we finally had found the conditions we were looking for.

We called the FAC and had the choppers start toward us. We had our two imposter guards get up as close as they could to the two guards we had picked. Within 5 minutes, both guards were down, dragged into the brush, and replaced by our people. We sent the Yard that had done the crossbow shooting back along the line of guards. He would wait until he saw the NVA NCO go down, then he would shoot the guard in front of him if he responded in any way.

At 0250 the NCO walked past our first imposter guard and was shot with a knockout dart. He went down with almost no noise. The team ran up and carried the NCO off into the brush. We gagged him, tied him up with duck tape on the stretcher, and took off for the pickup point. We had about 3 kilometers to travel in the next hour and thirty minutes. This would be tough because we were carrying dead weight on the stretcher. The medic made us stop once, when the prisoner seemed to be waking up. He quickly was put back down by the medic and we continued on.

We reached the extraction point for the prisoner about 5 minutes late. I immediately called the FAC and he said the chopper was holding about two miles out. I setup an infrared beacon in the small clearing, and told the FAC to send in the chopper. The chopper found us pretty quickly and dropped the penetrator down in the small clearing. We sat the prisoner on the legs of the penetrator and taped him up. We used almost all the tape we had. We didn't want him falling off during the two hour flight back to Nakhon Phanom.

It was time to head out for our extraction point about another 3 kilometers away. We reached the team extraction point and did a security sweep of the area. No NVA were there, and the two Yards that had impersonated the guards were waiting for us.

A call to the FAC confirmed that our ride home was about 15 minutes out. I confirmed a cold LZ as of that moment, and we prepared to get out of the area in one piece. The chopper called for us to give him a marker, and I put a beacon out in the LZ. Two minutes later we were boarding the chopper.

We were about 30 feet up in the air when the shooting started. A Huey has no armor around the passenger compartment. It was just thin gauge metal and holes were appearing in the wall and floor. A roving NVA patrol had happen by in hearing distance of the helicopter when it landed. They were firing at us and were preparing to fire an RPG when the door gunner saw it. The machine gun cut the man with the RPG down before he could fire, and the chopper made its way off to safety.

The NCO looked at me and asked how bad I was hurt. I looked at him without comprehending that he was talking to me. He stepped across the chopper floor and wiped the blood flowing down the back of my neck. It wasn't as bad as it looked. It was just a small scalp wound that bled enough to look like I was really hurt. I hadn't felt the bullet that grazed me, or even noticed the bleeding until the NCO brought it to my attention.

The medic with the team quickly got the bleeding stopped and I sat down suddenly feeling weak and scared. He assured me that it was not a problem, and that he had it under control. I just nodded to him, and leaned against the wall.

Two hours later we landed back at Nakhon Phanom. The medic made me go with him to the dispensary and get the wound properly cleaned and bandaged.

Thirty minutes later I was sitting in the TOC writing out a report to be sent to the shop. The prisoner had made it back just fine. He had been so scared that he had soiled himself, but otherwise was OK. It was one more trip to No-Man's-Land and just another day **<u>Inside the World of Mirrors.</u>**

Chapter 8
Cambodia Didn't Count

This was my second trip into South Vietnam. Of all the times I had been in Cambodia, Laos, and North Vietnamese, you might wonder how I had missed the opportunity for another all expense paid vacation to Charlie's back yard. The briefing was at MACV.

The 1300 briefing was at a military facility, but only two people in attendance were in uniform. The military personnel were Army Rangers, but not the ones I had worked for on my last trip. One was a Major and the other a Captain. They looked a little out of place amid the rest of the suits and tropical wear.

The primary briefer was a scruffy looking character right out of some silly movie about the Orient. I soon learned that he had been in country for about 10 years. Getting that appearance had produced the knowledge that he was presenting now.

Someone in the Intelligence community had discovered that a high ranking NVA officer was going to be coming down the trail to visit the mountain tunnel hospitals in Cambodia. Up till now, only SIO had been in Cambodia.

The intelligence information told us that sometime during a 5 day period, this officer would be riding down the trail. The mission was to infiltrate an area of the trail that was in between two large mountains. The NVA had built an underwater bridge across a river that was between the mountains.

It was a single lane bridge, so traffic always backed up there. The Air Force had tried many times to knock out the bridge, but had been badly beaten up by all the anti-aircraft guns and hand held ground to air heat seeking missiles.

The Army Ranger Company represented at the meeting had been working near the area. It had been decided by someone up the line that this made them the primary members of a team to go into the area. In any event, I was going along for the ride to take the shot.

After an intensive briefing session, everyone but the briefer, the rangers, and I were dismissed. The briefer gave the Major a set of maps and paperwork.

The paperwork had no identification on it. The briefer gave a phone number to call if we needed any special equipment and turned us loose to go back to the Ranger's base in the highlands.

I went downstairs and got my gear that I had left with the Security Detail. Then we hopped in a jeep and headed for the air base. An hour later we were in the air in a Huey for the 90 minute flight to their camp.

By the time we reached the camp, it was well after dark. The mess was closed, so they just took me to the TOC, where I left the majority of my gear with Security, and then to a tent with a cot for me. They said chow was at 0630, and that we would meet at the chow hall. With past experience as a guide, I immediately went to bed to get all the rest I could before the fun and games began again.

The next morning came much too soon, but I was at the mess hall at the appointed time. The captain was there and walked me through the mess line and over to a set of tables in the back of the mess hall. There were only two people in the back area. Both were senior NCOs (Non-Commissioned Officers). I was introduced and we sat down and ate.

The discussion was held in quiet tones. No one closer than 15 feet could have understood anything we said. The questions initially were directed at my background and experience, because they were rightfully worried about going into the bad bush with someone who didn't know what it was about. I had no problem with the questions, and they relaxed after I told them that South Vietnam was somewhat new to me, but that 21 missions into Cambodia, Laos, and North Vietnam missions comprised all my experience in the theater. We finished eating breakfast in silence.

This mission would be a bit different for me. I usually was in country for no more than 36 hours before I went to the field. This time our mission profile started in 5 days.

We went to the TOC, and discussed the mission. They brought in lunch, and we kept right on working. The key issue was how close we would need to get for me to be able to make the hit. I told them that I would prefer to work no more than 600 meters out, but had been successful as far as 1100 meters. I made sure that they understood that the longer distance was with perfect conditions and virtually no wind.

They asked to see me shoot, which was a reasonable request, so we went out to their firing range. They were really surprised when I pulled out my LC-1A, attached the scope, and loaded up. They were surprised because it was such a strange looking weapon. It had 23" of barrel beyond the stock, and was supported by a bi-pod for firing stability. In addition it was a single shot weapon. When asked, I told them that my best time from shot to shot had been on the range at the Farm. At 600 meters, I put 6 rounds in the bull's eye in 59 seconds. They looked at me as if I was totally nuts. I could tell that they didn't believe me.

I just asked what target they wanted me to shoot at. They pointed at a small metal target about 500 yards away. It was about two feet wide and 4 feet tall.

I got into position to fire and told them to time me starting from when I fired the first shot. I had 5 rounds lying on a field pack next to me, and one round already chambered in the LC-1A. I took my time getting comfortable and properly set up with a good sight picture.

I exhaled and pulled the trigger back to the arming point, took one more breath, exhaled, and applied more pressure to the trigger. The weapon fired. I never took my eye away from the scope. I ratcheted the spent casing out and put in another round. I fired again, and repeated the process till all six rounds had been fired.

I stood up, looked at the Captain that had come out with us, and asked how I did. He had been watching the target with binoculars. He said the target moved each time I shot, but of course he couldn't tell where the rounds had hit.

I picked up my equipment, and we walked down range to the target. I had to apologize, as only 5 rounds were in the bull's eye, but the 6th round was only about 2 inches outside of the bull's eye. They laughed when I apologized, and said it was apparent that I would do just fine.

I went over to the armory, cleaned my weapon, and left my gear there under lock and key. The only weapon I kept with me was my 22 berretta with the silencer attached.

We then went to the mess hall and had dinner. I'll say one thing for the Rangers' mess hall, they took really good care of their troops. The food was surprisingly tasty. Over dinner we discussed a short practice mission in a relatively safe area, just so we could get used to working together.

I agreed, and we planned a patrol that would last only one night in the field. We would go in tomorrow about 1700. After dinner they took me to the NCO club, and we had a couple of beers. Then it was off to bed.

We met the next afternoon at 1630 at the armory, and walked over to the pad. The chopper was waiting, so we got in and took off. We landed, and went directly to the edge of the bush.

We had already agreed upon the formation, so I was down with my AK-47 pointed in the right direction. My LC-1A case and scopes were strapped to my back, and my 22 berretta with silencer was attached to my pistol belt. After about 5 minutes, they motioned for me to take point. I took a compass bearing, picked a tall tree, and started moving toward it. They let me get about 20 steps ahead then followed after me. I never went near the trail. Instead I went well up hill before I started toward our objective. I would stop and listen for a minute, then move about 10 steps, and stop and listen again. This continued until we reached the first tree we had sighted on. We had only moved about 200 meters, but it had taken me almost 30 minutes to get there.

We pulled up in a dense area of bush, and another ranger was put on point. When we reached the objective, we set up our RON (Rest-Over-Night) and set the watch pattern. They did not use the circle technique I was used to, but they were well disciplined otherwise.

They certainly moved well in the bush. The next morning we worked our way back to the LZ for to be picked up. They were somewhat casual about checking the security of the area around the

LZ. I let it pass, and when the chopper landed, we got in and went back to camp.

We agreed to meet again after lunch. I cleaned my weapons, even though they had not been fired. I even cleaned the scope covers before I put them on again.

After lunch they said that I moved well in the bush, but was a little slow. I responded by telling them that they moved too fast for Cambodia. The enemy was much thicker there than anywhere in South Vietnam, in some areas a square mile might contain 2000 or 3000 NVA.

I made it clear to them that we were not going to be moving more than 2 kilometers per hour in Cambodia. Since I had been there, they politely nodded their heads in agreement.

Then I explained about the circle mode that I wanted to use at night in our RON. When I explained about the string tied between us and how it was used to warn members of the team that a potential threat was near, they agreed to do it my way.

The last point I made was about how I was trained to check out the area around the LZ. I explained why I carried a 22 berretta with a silencer and four 5 round magazines. When I was finished, they were much more sober that when we began. I told them that they knew what to do, but in Cambodia, we needed to be more careful and move a little slower.

We met again after dinner, and they told me that they had two Montenyards that they worked with that would be going with us. I said fine, but how many rangers would be going. When they said they normally worked in teams of 6 men, I flinched.

I told them there is no way to move covertly in Cambodia with more that 4 or 5 people total. They said they would have to talk with the Captain about that. I said go do it now, because I'm not going into Cambodia with 8 or 10 people.

I was not going to commit suicide or get a bunch of people killed if I could avoid it. They shook their heads in puzzlement, but left to talk to the Captain.

The Captain came back and asked me to join him at the Major's hooch. We walked over, and I repeated everything I had said to the team, and embellished on the reasons for it. When I was finished, the Major looked at me for what seemed to be a long time.

Then he said he understood why they sent me and asked if I would spend a few minutes to outline a training program that he could use with his people. I agreed to his request then restated that 5 team members was the absolute maximum number of personnel for the mission. He nodded his agreement, shook hands with me, and said it's your mission, and we'll do it your way.

I felt flattered that he had responded as he did, but I also felt the terrible weight of command drop on my shoulders. I nodded and the Captain led me out to his tent.

I strongly recommended that we take one Montenyard because the crossbow they carried could be useful to get us out of trouble. Then I said I would prefer only two of his rangers because of the better movement capability, but would accept three if he insisted.

He said the Major had picked five men, and we would meet with them now, and pick three of them to go. I really did not like this situation, because it seemed that I was being asked to choose who would get a chance to die.

We met with the five Rangers, and after some discussion, I offered three of them the opportunity to come on the mission. We would go in tomorrow and begin the approach to the target over a two day period.

I gave them a full briefing on how we would operate, and they all agreed. I asked if any of them had a silenced weapon. One did, and I asked him to bring it with him. Extra firepower that was quiet could be a major advantage.

We met the next afternoon at the appointed time, boarded the chopper, and took off. It was a long flight to the LZ. When I got the five minute warning, I looked at my watch. We were almost 40 minutes late.

This would mean almost total darkness within a few minutes of our landing. This was not a good way to start off. If the LZ was hot you would buy the farm. If it was cold, you would have difficulty get orientated and moving out.

As we were descending into the LZ we started receiving incoming fire. We had a hot LZ. I grabbed the microphone and told the pilot to get us out of here.

He went back up and headed toward our alternate LZ. We hit the alternate LZ and it was cold. Well, one thing had sort of worked anyway. We ran to the edge of the bush, and set up to see if we were about to meet some company.

After 10 minutes, the radio operator called the chopper with a Code Green message. That told the chopper to go home, and that we were down and moving out.

I pointed at the Montenyard. Then pointed a direction I had taken from my compass to move. The Montenyard was good in the bush. Hell, all of the hill people were good in the bush. They had lived in it all their lives.

We moved about 3 kilometers when I signaled a back trail check. We looped around and moved into some heavy brush. After few minutes, I told them to take a five minute break.

When we took off again, I pointed the direction for the Montenyard and he led us off. We followed about 20 meters behind him. The senior Ranger NCO was walking trail and watching the back door. I was in the middle of the line as we moved. After another 2 kilometers, I signaled a back trail check again.

We looped around and moved into some very dense brush about 0400. This would be a good hide for us. I set up the watch schedule, we moved into our defensive circle, and passed the day quietly.

At 1900 we loaded up and continued the approach. This time we went much slower. We were in Charlie's back yard. I had no intention of disturbing the residents.

We reached our next check point about 30 minutes behind schedule, which was excellent because the chopper insertion to the alternate LZ had caused us to be so much later than we expected.

We had moved quietly and quickly without contact. So far it was all according to plan. We moved until 2300, when I signaled for a back trail check again. We looped around and up the hill into some light bush. Ten minutes later it appeared that no one was hot on our trail yet.

So we set off for the next check point. At 0300 I signaled another back trail check, and we looped around and up to the top of the hill into very dense brush. This would be our hide for the coming day.

I then set up a watch rotation, and the senior Ranger NCO and I slipped out and over the top of the hill. We had done much better than I expected. We had moved at night through strange bush, and had come within about 300 meters of where we had decided to try the hit.

The Sergeant and I slowly moved down to the preselected site, and, as usual, found that while the cover was good, the line of sight for the shot was not.

We moved about 50 meters further down the hill side toward the river and found an excellent observation and shooting position in very deep brush. We agreed that this was the spot, and went back to our team hide. I pulled everyone in tight, and gave them a quick brief on what and where. Then we set up a movement into position for 0400 the next day and went to sleep.

We moved out as planned and settled in to wait out the day. We only saw one patrol during the day, and they were pretty casual. They had walked the trail below us many times before, so they were certain nothing was wrong. I only hoped that they would stay that way. The day passed with no sign of the target. At 1900 we moved back to our hide position.

We moved out on schedule the next morning. I left the Montenyard and two Rangers in our original planned position, and the senior NCO and I again moved up to the firing position. I was setup and ready in about 5 minutes. Then we waited for our target.

The day passed without sighting our target, and we retraced our steps back to the hide we had used last night. We set up the watch schedule with a planned return to the forward positions at 0400 again.

Back in position the next morning, we started the observation again. I was my turn on the binoculars when the car arrived. I gave them to my partner and he agreed that this was our target. The target wasn't close enough to the river crossing for me to take the shot.

The NCO got back on the glasses to watch again. We had been observing casual patrolling by the enemy since we had been here, but that suddenly changed.

They were starting to patrol much further up the mountain sides on both sides of the river. It became apparent that in about an hour, they would be very close to our current position. We had no choice but to move back further away till they went past.

We also moved the security team back with us. We were now about 900 meters out from the bridge, and about 200 meters higher than the crossing area. The distance and difficulty of the shot was much tougher than the original position.

When we were set up again, the Ranger NCO told me that the traffic pattern on the road had changed, and that the car was approaching the crossing much sooner than we expected.

I immediately set up to get a good sight picture. This was a difficult shot to attempt under normal conditions. It was a shot through winds that would swirl in the canyon. Our chances of a good clean shot had decreased substantially.

The choice was never as clear as you always heard it said. It was a matter of honor. I thought to myself that it might be the death of us, but I was taking the shot.

The Ranger NCO went back to the binoculars and readied himself to help me adjust the fire. I pulled the trigger to the arming position, and slowly applied more pressure. The shot went off and echoed through the canyon. The ranger told me I was 2 feet high and 3 feet to the right.

By the time he had it said, I had reloaded and was adjusting the scope. I fired again, and he said "Oh God, Let's go!" He pulled me to my feet and we took off at a run.

As we were running I gasped out to him, did I hit him? He replied, "You tore out the back of his pants." What a scar that would leave!

By then we had had picked up the rest of the team and the running war began. The enemy was coming from every direction. We were in a fierce fire fight with the first squad to reach us.

We just opened up with our AK-47s and each of us shot off a full magazine at the squad. Then we were off and running in a different direction. This went on for what seemed to be forever. No thought was given to escape. We just insanely charged every group of enemy troops we met.

Sometime late in the afternoon, I realized that there were only 3 of us now. The Montenyard, the Senior Ranger NCO, and I were all that was left of the team.

We had run out of the ammunition we had brought with us and had been stripping magazines off the bodies of the people we killed. Then we would take off again till we met the next group of enemy troops.

We had survived to this point by attacking the enemy we met as if we were rabid dogs. No thought was given to survival. We only wanted to kill as many as we could.

All three of us had minor wounds. My wound was just a scratch. But it was a strange scratch. A bullet had entered the helmet at such an angle that it just curved around inside the helmet and came out again. It was not life threatening, but was a problem because of the light bleeding.

In the next engagement, we killed 5 more enemy soldiers, grabbed their magazines, and I was ready to take off again when I realized that the Senior Ranger NCO was on the ground.

He had been ripped wide open across his abdomen. There was no chance we could save him, and he knew it.

I shall never forget his last request. "Pull the pins out of two grenades, put them in my hands, and roll me over face down. When they find me, I'll kill some more!"

I did as he asked. I had no idea what I was going to do next. I waved to the Montenyard, and we started moving away. About 20 minutes later we heard the grenades go off. We just kept walking, no longer running, just waiting for the next group of enemy soldiers to finish our little war.

It was now after dark, and we finally realized that somehow we had broken contact with the enemy. We had no idea where we were, or how we got there.

We moved into a dense stand of elephant grass, and just lay down. Just as dawn was breaking, the Montenyard woke me up. I was amazed that we were alive. Our only chance was to go east.

So we walked at night, and slept in the day, for what seemed like forever. The Montenyard found berries and water for us as we went. This went on till he found a Montenyard village, which, luckily for us, had Green Berets living with them.

They took us in, and hid us away until we regained some measure of composure. It was virtually impossible that we had lived through what had just occurred, but here we were.

About 4 days later a chopper came in with military supplies for the village. They took me out with them. The Montenyard stayed in the village.

We landed at a Green Beret camp, and I was transferred to a medivac (Medical Evacuation) chopper to Saigon. After that I was on Air America flight to Japan, and a C-130 to Korea.

I never saw the Ranger camp again. I would never be able to tell them what had happened. This was my last mission involved with the Vietnam Conflict. They knew better than try to send me back. They knew I wouldn't go. I still hold the shame and pain within me. It will never go away.

Many years later, I went to see the Vietnam Wall traveling memorial. I looked for the names of the Rangers, the Marines, and the Green Berets that I had worked with, but could not find any of them on the wall.

I went to the information stand, and asked them where the names were. They said they had no such names listed. I said that I was with them when they died in Cambodia, Laos, and North Viet. I was told that deaths in question were not in the "Theater of War."

It was a Vietnam Memorial. I broke down and cried. I still can't believe that none of the deaths in Cambodia, Laos, and North Vietnam were counted.

<u>NONE OF US COUNTED!</u>

I still see them from time to time as we meet every
so often in my nightmares. Once again, I relive
the tragedies and the horrors we went through.
They may not have counted officially, but I was
in command. I was responsible for them.

<u>They will not be forgotten
for as long as I live.</u>

Chapter 9
A Visit to an Irish Pub

The phone rang about 1800. I was sitting in my comfortable recliner waiting for Sunday Night Football to start. The Washington Redskins were playing the Dallas Cowboys, and the winner would be leading the division.

I picked up the phone, and was told that a car would come to pick me up at 2000. What wonderful timing! The game would be about half over, and I wouldn't get to see the rest of the game.

At 1955 I walked out to the front curb. The car was already waiting for me, so I got in and the driver took off. We arrived at the shop about 2045. I walked in the front door, and was escorted to the main briefing room.

Woody Woodford was waiting for me along with two strangers. I sat down and Woody introduced the strangers as Mike and Steve.

I knew those weren't their real names. I just nodded to the two strangers, and poured myself a cup of coffee. Woody began the briefing with a surprising statement. The mission was planned for Northern Ireland. I had never worked in an allied country before.

The Irish Republican Army (IRA) was causing trouble again. The IRA used the area around South Armagh as their headquarters. This was a tight knit farming area, and all strangers were looked on as a threat. The Special Air Service (SAS) personnel were working the area just south of the border of Northern Ireland, and were trying to slow down the infiltration of IRA terrorists.

They needed an observer to let them know when a certain individual was not at his favorite pub. It had been noticed by British intelligence that if this person was not at the pub, then a cross border mission by terrorists would happen during the night. They had been using personnel from MI-6 (British Foreign Intelligence Service) to keep a discreet surveillance of the pub until last week.

They were notified by MI-6 that the agent doing the surveillance had ceased communication. They had assumed that the IRA had kidnapped him. They wanted me to take a vacation, and replace the missing agent. It would also be nice if I could find out where he was being kept.

I asked why they thought that he was still alive, and was informed that the IRA would kidnap people and try to trade them for their people who were in British jails. If no trade was worked out, the kidnapped individuals just disappeared. No contact indicating a possible trade had occurred, so the SAS thought that he was still being held for use later.

I would be posing as a tourist. I would actually arrive on a tourist bus. Then I would get sick, and the bus would leave me behind.

I told them that this seemed to be an obvious way to make me a target. It was very thin on credibility, and had no backstopped documentation to prove I wasn't working for MI-6 or the SAS. I told them that if I decided to take on the mission, I would determine how I got there, and build my own cover story. They were unhappy, as they were used to telling people what to do.

They provided me maps of the area, along with pictures and information on Rodney McDougal, the target subject that they wanted observed.

I asked them where the individual in question lived, and they said that they didn't know. They thought he was a low level messenger. All they knew was that he lived within a short distance, because he always came to the pub on a bicycle.

I told them that this conclusion was not necessarily based on reality. If he lived close enough to ride a bicycle then their previous agent would have found out where he lived. I told them that I believed that the bicycle was a false flag, and that the subject's residence would be the first item necessary to know. They were so irritated with me that Woody suggested that we take a break, and took me down the hall to his office.

Woody told me to "take it easy" on our allies. Then it occurred to me that some heavy political pressure was being brought on the SAS by the British government. I told Woody of my suspicions, and he just smiled and shook his head in agreement.

I told Woody that if I was to take this mission, it would be done under our plans, and for our reasons. I wasn't going blindly into a situation that had already caused one person to disappear.

He excused himself, and went back to Mike and Steve. He told them to come back tomorrow evening, and we would try to have something solid to discuss with them. Then he returned to his office, and we started brain storming on what should be done, and how it should be handled.

I told him that I didn't believe that MI-6 had the right name for the target. In addition, I didn't believe that the individual in question was a low level runner for the IRA. If every time he disappeared a terrorist attack took place, then I felt that he was much higher up in the power structure in the IRA.

I suggested that he was either a major cell leader, or a bomb maker. In either case, we had a more important target than the SAS and MI-6 thought. Then I told Woody that I suspected that MI-6 had a mole in it that had access to the SAS chain of operations.

Steve had told us that they rarely were successful in their attempts to catch terrorists crossing the border. They would catch minor runners, and others of that level, but had never caught a major player or large group.

I suggested that we get MI-5 (British Intelligence working in England only) to run a background check of the SAS personnel in planning and operations and see who had relatives or close friends in Northern Ireland.

It was just too much of a coincidence that only small players were being caught while crossing the border. Somebody had to know where the SAS field personnel were going to be.

Woody went to check what flights were available to get me to Northern Ireland as quickly as possible. He found an Air Force C-5 that was scheduled to leave Andrews at 0100 in the morning, and get me on the ground well before the meeting with Mike and Steve was scheduled.

I called the Farm on a secure line, and ordered a number of

special cameras and listening devices, along with my 22 caliber pistol with a silencer and 50 rounds of subsonic ammunition to be delivered to me at Andrews Air Force Base before takeoff.

I didn't need to go back home and get my clothes, as I always had several sets of travel clothing in the basement at the shop.

I grabbed up my suit case and several passports with matching credit cards, and went out the door. The driver was waiting, and we left for Andrews Air Force base. I got there about an hour before scheduled takeoff, and met the delivery from the Farm.

It was all in a large, well-used suitcase. Then we loaded up, and flew to a secure air base in Northern England.

Upon landing, I was taken to a car rental company, and picked up a car. Then I went back to the air base and took both suitcases, loaded them in the car, and took off on the M1 for Northern Ireland.

I arrived in South Armagh late in the afternoon, and checked into the hotel where the pub was located. I saw our target in the pub, and went to the restaurant for dinner. Then I went into the Pub for a quick drink. The barkeeper told me they closed up about 2300. I had another drink and went to my room.

At 0100, I quietly slipped out of my room and went down stairs to the pub. Nobody was around, so I took three of the tiny optic cameras, each about the size of a pencil, and set them up on top of the books in the bookcases. Then I ran a wire between each camera to a special radio transmitter which I had hidden among the books on the top row.

I felt very comfortable that the cameras and transmitter would not be found, because the books on the bookcase were covered in dust. The radio transmitter had a battery capable of running for 24 hours without being replaced. Each camera ran off the radio transmitter's battery. I ran an antenna line along the back of the top row of books.

I could receive transmissions from as far as a mile away, so I didn't have to stay at the hotel. Then I went back up stairs to my room. The transmitter was set up to work off a timer. It would transmit for 3 hours each night from 1900 to 2200. I went to bed, and set the alarm for 0900.

In the morning, I checked out of the hotel, and drove away. I went about a half mile, and turned into another hotel. I was in luck, and they had a room available for the next 7 days. I made arrangements and prepaid the bill for the week.

I then left and drove about 20 kilometers to a train station. I knew that I could find a telephone there. I called the shop, through a number I had been given in London, and told the operation monitor that I was having a wonderful time, and expected to enjoy the sights for about a week.

I then hung up, asked for directions to an excellent restaurant, and went to eat. After a wonderful lunch, by British standards, I went back to my hotel and went to sleep.

At 1900 I turned on my receiver equipment, hung an antenna wire outside my window, and waited to see if our target came in. At approximately 2000, the target walked in, ordered a pint, and sat down in the corner talking with some other men.

I immediately turned off the receiver, pulled in the antenna wire, and went out to my car. I drove back near the pub with the transmitter and cameras, and started walking toward the pub. I was delighted to see only one bicycle in front of the building.

In the hopes that it was the one my target rode, I walked by, and casually attached a miniature radio transmitter under the seat of the bicycle. I then walked away. I found a place to park the car that gave me a clear view of the bicycle.

About 2130, my target came out, got on the bicycle, and rode away. The transmitter under the seat of the bicycle would send an electronic signal 3 times each minute. I had a receiver display with a circular antenna. When the transmitter would send its signal, the receiver display had an arrow that pointed toward the source of the signal.

This transmission was powerful enough to send the signal up to three miles away. As the beep changed the arrow direction, I pulled out and headed in that direction. It was headed out to the east, so I slowly followed to avoid overtaking the bicycle.

Several cars came toward me from the other direction, and passed by as would normally be expected. Approximately 2 minutes later, the arrow suddenly changed direction, and started pointing back behind me. That indicated that I had passed the bicycle. I found a small roundabout and came back toward the signal. This time I drove a little slower, while watching the arrow.

Suddenly the arrow pointed to my right, and then swung around to point behind me. That indicated that the bicycle was on the right side of the road, just behind where I was. I turned around and drove until the arrow swung around to the left.

I immediately pulled the car over and parked. I got out and casually strolled back to the street where the arrow had pointed. I stepped into the shadows cast by a building, and saw the bicycle leaning against the wall.

I walked over, reached up under the seat to remove the bug, and quickly walked back to my car. I was almost done for the night. All I had to do was find a location where I could watch the bicycle tomorrow but not be seen.

I quietly drove around the area, but found no place that let me see but not be seen. I started driving back toward my hotel when I saw a small park with lots of bushes and trees. I drove around the behind the park, and found a place to leave my car. I walked into the park, and after several minutes found a place that I could see the street, but would not be easily seen.

Now I had a plan of action. I would arrive back at the park and leave my car where it was not visible from the street. Then I would sit on a park bench and pretend to read a book. I would start my vigil about 1600, and if I saw the rider and bicycle go by, I would go to the location where I had found the bike. If there was a car there I would attach the directional bug to it. With my mind made up, I went back to the hotel and went to bed.

I slept till 1300 the next day. I cleaned up, changed clothes, and went to eat a lunch near the park. I got to my park bench about 1600. I was there much earlier than was probably necessary, but my adrenaline was starting to flow. I was closing in on my target.

It was a long quiet wait, but finally the rider passed by on the road about 1800. I went to my car and drove back to the area where the bicycle had been last night.

I parked the car and walked from there down the street past the location where the bicycle had been. I was pleased to find a green Volvo parked next to that area. I walked on by, and when I was sure no one was paying any attention to me, I turned and walked back to the car.

I wrote down the make, model, and license number, put the directional beeper under the back bumper of the car, and walked back to my car.

I drove the back to the train station and called my number in London. I gave them the information, and said I would call back in an hour or so. I walked across the street from the train station and had dinner in a small café.

When the hour was up, I went back to the train station and again called the London number. They gave me the owner's name, address, and phone number. He was listed in the phone book.

I now knew that Patrick O'Conner was probably his real name. I drove back to the park and sat waiting for the bicycle to come back by.

Around 2200 the rider returned on the bicycle. I hurried to my car, and about 3 minutes later, the locator beeped and the arrow started moving. I went to my car, and started following the arrow. It was a short drive. The second road outside the city was a dirt road leading back into the farm lands. The arrow suddenly pointed down the road, then swung around to point behind me.

I drove on till I found a good place to quietly wait. The arrow had stopped moving. The bird had come to rest, and now I knew its favorite roost. As I sat there deciding what to do next, a large truck came driving down the road and turned into the dirt road that my target had taken. It was an open bed truck, and had 10 or 12 men in the back.

Alarm bells went off in my head. I got out of the car, took my pistol with the silencer attached and 3 extra five round magazines, and started walking across the field parallel to the dirt road. After about 10 minutes, I saw the lights of a house on the hill ahead of me.

I immediately moved further to the left off the road and went about on about 100 meters. Then I stopped, and just stared ahead. It's an old trick you use in the bush. You look straight ahead without blinking your eyes, and sooner or later the enemy will do something that will tell you where he is. After about 5 minutes, I had seen nothing so I walked for about 10 meters, stopped, and repeated the process. My training paid dividends. I saw a spark of light, then just the red glow of a cigarette.

The sentry was not really expecting anything, or anyone. He had probably done this many times, and nothing ever happened. For a small transgression such as this, he could die.

I worked my way around him and went on toward the house. There were no outside lights on the house, only the soft glow of the windows penetrated the dark night. I circled the house twice, but found no other enemy personnel.

I could hear laughter, and came closer to the window. I stood in the dark shadow and listened for about 15 minutes, then went back to my car. I drove immediately to the train station again, and called my London Number.

As soon as the phone was answered, I started talking, and gave a mini-debriefing of the actions to date. I told them where the terrorists were going to strike, and where they were going to cross the border. I also gave them a name . . . Davon.

This was the name of their contact who had told them where the SAS teams were going to be working. The listener on the other end of the phone said to call back at 1400 local time for further instructions. I hung up the phone and went back to my hotel.

I silently raged at the results that I had found. The target was a doctor with offices in the next village, and was known for his mild manner and kind ways. I wondered what would make a person show one face to the world in the light of day, and another at night. Then I realized that I did the same thing he did. I would show one face to the world, but would instantly switch to an operational mode with no second thoughts or regrets. We were the same only different.

I made the required call back through the London number and got new instructions. I repeated the instructions, and they were confirmed. I went to back to my hotel to wait.

Tomorrow night, the terrorists would be met by the SAS. Tomorrow night someone named Davon would be locked away somewhere by British authorities. Tomorrow night the Doctor might die, or then again, maybe not. It just depended on the way things worked out.

I went back to the hotel and went to bed. I was most likely going to need all the rest I could get. I spent the next day relaxing, and ate two meals. At 1900, I drove back toward the doctor's home. I found a place where I could park the car and not have it seen from the road.

Then I started walking toward the house. I went well out of my way to avoid the location that the sentry had been at last night. I was about 300 meters from the house, when I saw a group of men walk out of the house and get in the old flat bed truck. But this time, the truck had a tarp over the cargo area.

The truck started up and pulled away. When it got to the main road, it turned right and disappeared into the night. Then I worked back to the area where the sentry had been at last night.

It took about an hour, but I finally found him leaning against the same tree he was by last night. I backed away, and returned to the house comfortable that I knew where the possible trouble could come from.

I was only about 30 meters from the house when the door opened. The target came out carrying a large bag, and went around the back of the house with it.

I quickly moved up to the house and went inside. There was a small alcove just inside the door. The door opened up in such a way that the alcove was not immediately visible to someone entering the house.

I slipped into the alcove and waited for my target to return. After about 4 or 5 minutes, I began to worry that the target had gone somewhere. I had not heard a car start, but that didn't mean he hadn't used it. I was just about to step out of the alcove when the door handle turned and the door started to open. I waited until the door was about half open then pushed the door very hard to knock whoever was behind it off balance.

The door pushed the target back against the wall, and I stepped forward and hit him hard in the stomach. I then hit him again on the side of his face. He fell to the floor, and started to get up. I pushed my gun in his face and told him to freeze. He did not try to escape, but only lay on the floor staring at the gun.

I had him roll over on his stomach, and tied his hands behind his back with some thin wire I had brought with me. I then tied his feet together, and gagged him so he couldn't may a sound.

I rummaged around in his pockets, and found a set of car keys. I helped him stand up, then grabbed him from behind and dragged him out the door. I pulled him around the house where he had gone before, and found the Volvo parked next to a small shed.

I opened the trunk of the Volvo, and found the large bag he had carried out of the house. I put the bag in the back seat of the car and then forced him into the trunk. I started the car, and drove back toward the main road.

As I neared the location where I had found the sentry, I started to accelerate the car to a very fast speed. The sentry had stepped out on the dirt road, and had to jump just to keep from being run over.

By the time he got back on his feet, I was turning onto the main road. I drove back to where I had parked my car, moved the bag into the back seat, and the doctor into the trunk.

Then I drove away to the train station. I walked in and called my London number. Briefly told them what had happened, and said I would call back in an hour or so to get directions to where I could dump the accumulated subject matter with SAS or MI-5. I got back in the car, and headed back to the south bound highway toward the air base where I had landed.

Two hours later, I stopped at a roadside phone booth, and called the London number again. They told me to drive toward the base till I saw a small roadside car park on the left side of the road.

I was to wait there until a military truck pulled into the car park. The truck would flash its head lights twice, and I was then to get out of the car, unlock the trunk, and walk away from the car.

I followed the instructions, and drove toward the air base. I found the roadside car park and pulled in. In less than 30 minutes, a truck pulled in and flashed its headlights twice. I got out of the car, unlocked the trunk, and walked away.

The truck pulled beside my car, blocking my view of the car, and in less than 3 minutes, started up and drove away. The trunk of the car was closed and the bag was gone from the back seat.

I got back in the car and drove to the air base. Five hours later, a business jet landed, and I was taken to it. The jet refueled, and then took off to go back to the U.S. I was very tired, but satisfied. I had pulled off an improbable snatch job, in the heart of IRA country, and had gotten away with it. Just one more vacation trip **Inside the World of Mirrors**!

Chapter 10
A Tea Party in Khaddafi Land

The call came at 0330. I was sound asleep after a long night celebrating my birthday. The caller did not identify himself, but it was both unnecessary and normal. All he said was that a car would be by at 0430 to pick me up.

I acknowledged the time, and the caller hung up. All that I could think of was that the shop had a terrible sense of timing. I was standing at the curb when the car pulled up exactly on time. I got in the back seat, told the driver to go, and immediately went back to sleep. I knew I was going to need every minute of rest I could get.

The driver woke me up when we arrived and escorted me to the front door. Ten minutes later I was sitting in a briefing room with Woody Woodford.

Woody almost always my handled my primary briefings. As usual, he looked like something out of GQ magazine. I, on the other hand, looked and felt like a poor job of embalming. It was a hell of a way to start a new day.

Woody started the briefing by telling me about a terrorist camp in Libya. Information had come in telling us that Ruholla Zerouel, Khaddafi's man in charge of Terrorist Training, was going to visit the camp in 3 days. The camp was 30 kilometers inside Libya and about 90 kilometers north of Algiers.

Mike Wilson, a Senior Intelligence Analyst (SIA) walked into the room carrying a stack of Satellite Imagery. The camp consisted of 5 large tents. The largest tent was in the middle of the camp, and was surrounded on three sides by the other 4 smaller tents. A vehicle park was on the east side of the camp.

Mike estimated that there were approximately 50 to 60 terrorists in the camp. Kaddafi was becoming a major player in the terrorist business, and Woody told me that camp had been determined to be a "Clear and Present Danger"!

Supposedly the only person who could make that statement was the President of the United States. I had heard it often enough to take the statement with a grain of salt. The mission was to take the camp down, and if Ruholla was eliminated, then so much the better.

We sat down and talked for over 2 hours before the plan finally came together. I would have 4 ex-SAS members, now working the mercenary side of the business, as my team. They had done jobs for my organization in the past, and had a solid reputation. I would have 2 vehicles for the approach and evasion process. Each member of the team would have AK-47s with 300 rounds of ammunition.

In addition, I requested 10 Rocket Propelled Grenades (RPGs), 8 were for use in the attack on the camp, and the other 2 were insurance in case we ran into Khaddafi's roving border guards. The border guards had no set schedule, just a requirement that no one got in or out of Libya in their sector.

That was the good news. The bad news was that the border guards were very well trained and equipped, and we had to get by them twice, if everything else went according to plan.

Woody gave me approval to execute the mission plan and two hours later I was boarding a flight to Algiers via Orly in France.

About 48 hours later, I was doing the final fit out and briefing of my team. We loaded up and pulled out about 2000 heading north to our planned border crossing point. When we reached the border, we pulled well off the road and stopped.

I immediately set up an observation post. I pulled out an infrared viewing device (IVD). Now it was time to wait until we saw the border guards go by. Just after 0130 local time, we saw them drive by. We waited another 15 minutes to make sure that they were not coming back toward us on their patrol pattern. We then set off for the camp site.

We arrived at our attack jump off point at 0230, and loaded up. They were all professionals, so all I said was, "Let's do it!"

We approached on foot, with two of the team, designated Team

1, taking their 4 RPGs and moving to the north side of the camp. The other two team members, designated Team 2, set up southwest of the camp. My position would be on the southeast side of the camp with a clear view of the vehicle park.

```
                     Attack Diagram

                        North
         Team 1 Position

                        Tent2
            Tent1

West                Main Tent      Vehicle Park      East

            Tent 3
                      Tent 4

         Team 2 Position              Sniper Position

                        South
```

The plan called for Team 1 to fire 2 RPGs into both Tent 1 and Tent 2. Team 2 was to do the same to Tent 3 and Tent 4. As soon and they had fired their RPGs, they were to return immediately to the jump off point and prepare for the exfiltration.

I was in the Sniper position, and waiting for the anthill to explode. I was counting on the fact that the leaders in the main tent would immediately run for the vehicle park to make a getaway. Less than a minute after the RPGs exploded, Ruholla and several other men came out of the main tent and ran for the vehicle park.

During the entire time they were running to the vehicle park, I never had a clear shot at Ruholla. They got to the vehicle park and jumped in a small truck. Ruholla got in the passenger seat, and my shot was still blocked by the driver.

To stop the getaway, I immediately shot the driver. Blood

splattered on Ruholla, and he dove out of the truck and was hidden by the truck body.

I moved my attention to a man in the back of the truck bed that was getting an old 30 caliber machine gun ready to fire. To eliminate this danger, I shot the machine gunner, and then, for good measure, shot the tire on the front of the vehicle.

Everyone that was left alive had ducked behind the truck and was headed for another vehicle. I had no clear shot, so I decided it was time to beat feet. I met the team members back at our vehicles about 10 minutes later. We jumped in and took off.

It was time to turn on the IVD and start hunting for the border guards. With all the noise we had just made, they had to be coming back. I needn't have bothered with the IVD, for they were coming straight at the camp with their headlights on. It looked like the last 2 RPGs were going to be useful.

We stopped our vehicles, and got out behind them. About that time someone in the border guards saw us and they turned toward us firing as they came.

When they were within 100 meters, we fired 1 RPG at front border guard vehicle and hit it in the front of the motor housing. It went up in a mass of flame. The second border guard truck was following the first vehicle so closely that it ran into the back of the first vehicle. Then we fired our last RPG into the second vehicle. That took care of any further pursuit.

We jumped back into our vehicles, and took off for the border. About 2 kilometers from the border, the engine of one of the jeeps quit. With no other option, we all crowded into the one jeep still running and crossed the border without further action.

As we drove south we watched for another vehicle we could use. After about 15 kilometers we found a small hotel on the side of the road. It had 5 or 6 vehicles parked in front of it.

We drove by, and when no other vehicles were in sight, pulled off the road to the right and behind some bushes. I went with two of the SAS mercenaries back to the car park in front of the hotel.

One of them crawled up to an old Volvo, and found the door unlocked. Within 1 minute he had the engine running. We jumped into the car and took off back along the road toward where we had left the jeep.

When I questioned the driver how he had obtained the skills to hotwire cars he just shrugged and said something about a misspent youth.

We dropped off the SAS mercenary in the back seat to go to the jeep. When he was out of sight, we started driving slowly back toward Algiers. About 10 minutes later the jeep pulled up behind us and blinked its lights. We sped up to normal driving speed and continued toward Algiers.

Two hours later we were back in Algiers at the safe house. Two of the team members had minor scratches, but nothing serious. The medics went to work, and I went to clean up, change clothes, and get some food in me.

Later, as I was leaving, I went to each of the team members, and thanked them for getting their job done. Then it was off to the airport for a flight to DC via Orly in France.

Sixteen hours later I was sitting in the briefing room at "The Organization that didn't exist".

I felt the mission was somewhat of a failure because Ruholla had gotten away. During the debrief Woody said it looked like a good mission to him, and we would know more in a couple of days. I went home with a parting comment, "Don't call me, I'll call you."

It later turned out that about 40 of terrorists were WIA or KIA, and the camp was completely destroyed. I was done until the next call sending me back again **Inside the World of Mirrors**.

Chapter 11
Dancing in the Shadow of the Vatican

I was traveling to Rome. The mission was being held so tight that even Woody said he didn't know what it was for. All he had given me was a contact method.

I would be walking into this a little less prepared that I wanted, but that was nothing new. I was carrying four different passports with matching identification and credit cards for each.

When the plane landed in Rome, I picked up my shoulder bag and walked to the Italian immigration official. He asked my purpose in coming to Italy, I told him it was to spend time touring Rome, and the Vatican in particular. He stamped my passport and sent me on my way.

I could have had somebody meet me at the airport, but I wanted to be sure that I was not being tailed. I walked past the waiting row of taxis, and went to the bus transport desk.

I purchased a ticket on the bus to take me downtown to one of the main hotels. About halfway into town we ran into heavy traffic as I knew we would. With the bus stopped in traffic, I walked up to the front and told the driver that I wanted to walk a while, and he opened the door. I got off the bus, and stood at the curb until the bus started moving again.

When the bus was out of sight, I started the next step in making myself disappear. I walked about two blocks and found an entry to the Underground. I went in, purchased a ticket, and went down to the platform to wait for the next train to anywhere. I got on the first train, and carefully observed who got on with me.

At the next stop I got off. None of the people that had gotten on the train with me got off. I waited until another train came and got on. I noted who got on with me. At the next stop, I got off again. None of the people that got off were paying any attention to me. I waited about 2 minutes, then went upstairs and out of the Underground facility.

There was a line of taxi's waiting along the curb. I walked to the first taxi and got in. I told him to drive back toward the airport. I sat sideways in the back seat and watched the cars behind me. After about 2 miles, I was sure that nobody was on my tail. I told the cab driver to pull over, paid him with a small tip, and got out.

I started walking toward the east until the taxi had driven out of sight. I then turned around and walked along the street until I found a small hotel.

I went in and asked if they had a room available for about 10 days. They did, and I let them see a different passport than the one I had used at the airport. I paid for the room with an American Express Card using the same name as was on the Passport.

It was quickly handled and the bellman took me up to the third floor, down the hall, and opened the door to my room. He opened the drapes, and asked if I needed anything. I said no and gave him a reasonable tip as he left.

It appeared that I had no surveillance on me and was cleanly in country. I waited about 2 hours, then went down the stairs, and walked out a side door to an alley beside the hotel. Then I walked out to the street, and turned away from the hotel's front door. I didn't care what direction I was going. All I wanted to do was to find another hotel or restaurant with a coin operated phone.

I found a large restaurant, went into the bar, and ordered a drink. I casually looked around the room, and saw a coin operated phone on the back wall near some small tables. I walked over and memorized the phone number printed on the phone, then returned to the bar. I finished my drink, paid the bill and tip, and walked out of the restaurant. I walked back toward my hotel and found a coin operated public phone box.

I dialed the contact number that I had been given by Woody and a raspy voice said "Ciao". I said "I'm trying to reach Enrico". The voice replied "My name is Michael." I said, "Do you like soccer?" He said "Only during the playoffs".

With this exchange the contact validation was complete and the raspy voice said "I expected your call earlier." I told him I did a little sightseeing and dry cleaning, and was ready to go to dinner. He gave me an address, said one hour, and hung up the phone.

I waved down a taxi, and gave him the address. Twenty minutes later we arrived at a small restaurant. I paid the bill, tipped the driver, and got out. I walked about 10 feet past the door to the restaurant and stopped. I lit a cigarette, and in less than 10 minutes a man walked up and asked for a light for his cigarette. He called me by the name I used coming through immigration.

As we walked down the street he told me that we were going to be meeting in a second floor apartment in about 30 minutes. To pass the time, we turned into another small restaurant and ordered a drink.

After about 30 minutes, a man came into the restaurant and walked up to our table. He called me by the name on the passport that I had used at immigration. I got up and we all walked out of the restaurant and went around the corner. We immediately turned into an apartment building, and walked up to the second floor. We turned right down the hall and stopped at the last door on the left. He put in a key, opened the door and we walked in.

A very well-dressed man was waiting on the couch. He stood up and was introduced as Mr. Martin. I knew very well that he was really a high level official at the American Embassy. I nodded and sat down in a chair facing him. He sat down and began talking.

He told me that there was no need to worry. He had the apartment sprayed for bugs every week, and in fact the workmen had just been here an hour ago. He was telling me that there were no electronic bugs in the room that he didn't know about. I nodded my head again, and he began the briefing.

He handed me a thick folder and said that there was a particular individual that was causing a serious problem right now. Local elections were coming up in two months, and this person was spreading around a lot of money to help get the communist candidates elected. He was in fact a bag man for the KGB.

I looked through the folder. It contained several pictures of the man, his name, address, and a lot of other information. I looked back at Mr. Martin and asked, "What do you need me for? " He said, "You must convince him to stop permanently, and I don't care how you do it".

He stood up, put on his coat, and headed for the door. Just before he opened the door to leave he turned around, looked straight at me, and said, "Anytime in the next week will be acceptable!" Then he opened the door and walked out.

I had just been told to kill a man I had never seen or heard of. At the Farm they called it "Pest Control", but what it really came down to was an assassination. If I got caught, they would deny any knowledge of me or my activities. I was an expendable pawn in the U.S Government's game of life. It was business as usual.

I turned to my initial contact and asked if the number I called was good 24 hours a day? He said yes. Then he asked for a number to contact me. I gave him the number of the restaurant's coin operated phone, and told him I could be reached at that number exactly at 2120 or 2340 each evening, and that the call must come exactly at that time.

He asked me what time it was, and I told him what my watch showed. He adjusted his watch to match mine, nodded his head, and walked out the door.

The man who had picked us up at the restaurant took me into the bedroom, and opened a large chest. It was full of large selection of guns, ammunition, and knives. Each gun was equipped with a silencer, and about half the knives had 6" or longer blades.

I put on a pair of thin leather gloves that I had brought with me, and began to look through the chest. I selected a 22 caliber berretta with silencer, three extra magazines of ammunition, and a switch blade knife with a 4" blade. I nodded my head and walked out of the apartment.

I walked down the street and caught a cab to my hotel. I went up to my room, and sat down to think things over. I had killed many people before, but this was the first time I was going one on one in a friendly nation. It took a while to get a grip on it.

It came down to being a shadow warrior to the end. My country's enemies were my enemies. With that thought, I turned and picked up the wooden desk chair, leaned it against the door, shut off the light, and went to bed.

The next morning, I called room service, and had breakfast brought up. After the waiter arrived and left me with my food, I picked up the folder and began an in-depth study of the material.

Included in the material was a map of the area around the target's residence. He lived almost in the shadow of Saint Peter's square. How ironic that a KGB bag man was living within spitting distance of the Vatican!

Supposedly, he had been observed for several weeks by a surveillance team, and his schedule was erratic during the day, but almost never changed after 1900.

He always walked east from his residence on Via Della Conciliazione, turning northeast on Plazza Pia, then north on Piazza Adriana, and finally back west to a restaurant on Via Crescenzio.

He would stay at the restaurant for about 3 hours then return home following a simple reverse of his pattern. Only two times in the last three weeks had the pattern varied. In both cases, it had been raining, and he had taken a cab to the same restaurant.

I was struck with the consistency of his movements. Either he loved the food, or one of his major contacts met him there. I expected to find that the second option was true.

I was concerned because not once had anyone mentioned having dinner in the restaurant to observe his activities. My first activity was to take a cab to the Saint Peter's Square. Then I followed Via Crescenzio east until I saw the building where he lived. I noticed that a small café with sidewalk tables was almost directly across the street.

I continued to follow his pattern of movement. It only took 15 minutes to walk briskly from his residence to the restaurant. I looked at the menu posted outside the restaurant, then reversed the trip back to his residence.

I noted only two areas that might not be well-lighted at night. I would have dinner tonight in the restaurant and see whom he was meeting.

I walked across the street to the small café across from his building, ordered a coffee, a pastry, and sat down to pass the afternoon. I saw him leave his residence once, but he immediately got in a taxi and took off. About 90 minutes later he returned. This time he came walking from the direction of the underground station.

As soon as he had entered the building, I paid my bill, and hailed a taxi, and went back to my hotel.

I had the hotel make reservations in the restaurant at 1900 and went up to my room. I changed into a dark English cut business suit. Now I would look different from my original appearance.

At 1800 I took a taxi to the restaurant, paid my fare, and walked in. I nodded to the man at the desk, and walked into the bar. I told the bartender that I had reservations at 1900, but would like a glass of white wine while I waited. I observed the traffic flow, and noticed a large table in an alcove in the back of the main room with drapes to provide privacy.

At precisely 1900, a waiter came to me and asked if I would like to be seated now. I agreed, and was taken to a table along the left wall of the dining room. I took a seat facing the front door, ordered a bottle of wine, and perused the menu.

It was obvious that the restaurant was set up to serve a wide variety of clients. The menu had each selection described in Italian, English, and French. I ordered dinner, and waited to see what would develop.

About 1940 the target walked in the door, but to my dismay, he had a rather large man with him. From the loose cut of his suit jacket, I surmised that he was carrying a pistol, and was a body guard. The surveillance reports had said nothing of this. In addition, the target was carrying a black brief case. I wondered what else they had not included.

My target was led to the table in the alcove, the curtains were closed, and the body guard stood outside the curtains. Within 20 minutes, another man was led into the curtained room. He wore a very expensive Italian suit, but his shoes were old and well worn. I had finished dinner, and was ready to order dessert when the second man came out of the alcove and left the restaurant.

I finished dessert, paid my bill, and went back to the bar and positioned myself to continue the surveillance of the alcove. At 2100 another man was led to the curtained alcove. I paid my bill, and left the restaurant.

I walked down to the corner, crossed the street, and came back up toward the restaurant. Within 20 minutes, the second man, came out and got in a taxi. I watched from a shadowed alley as people came and went at the restaurant. They had plenty of customers come into the restaurant. However, only once during the rest of the evening had any single person entered the restaurant without being with someone.

Within 30 minutes he had come back out. He also left quickly in a taxi. I had been in one place far too long. Someone might have noticed me, so I started to stroll back toward his residence.

I found a small café, and went in. I requested a table by the window, and was promptly seated. I ordered a small pastry and coffee, and waited. My back was toward the restaurant where I had eaten. I could not see them coming, but I could see them going by.

This was perfect, as I could get a feel for their timing, but they would not see my face unless they stopped right in front of the café and looked in. After about another 20 minutes, the target and his body guard came walking by. I paid my bill, and walked out the door.

I stood in the doorway until they were about 100 feet in front of me. Then I started walking after them. The body guard always stayed between the street and my target. He would occasionally glance up and back like he was checking for traffic to cross the street.

I crossed the street when he was not looking, and continued to follow them. When they turned onto his street where he lived, I walked in the opposite direction.

Something strange was going on. None of this important information had been included in my briefing package. I hailed a cab, and went back to my hotel.

I walked down the street to my restaurant with the coin operated phone. I took a table next to the phone, and had another coffee and pastry. I waited until the 2340 contact period passed, then paid my bill and went back toward my hotel. I paused twice as I walked, looking in store windows as if I were interested in what they had on display. I was really checking my back trail to see if anyone was following me. I detected no tail, so I went on to my hotel and to my room.

There was only one area that now met my criteria for my contact with the target. It was a side street where the nearest street light was far enough away to leave a large shadowed area where I could hide. If I was going to complete the mission, this was probably the place it would happen.

I moved the desk chair against the door and put the silenced pistol on the pillow beside me. I looked at the information folder and shook my head and went to bed. It took a while to go to sleep. There was something I couldn't put my finger on, but the puzzle was missing some important pieces.

Late the next morning, I put in colored contact lens, tinted my hair with a red tinged rinse, and combed my hair with a part down the middle. I went to the public phone down the street from my hotel. I called my original contact number, and simply told them I needed a meeting set up. I told them that I would call back in 1 hour to find out where the meeting would be. Then I hung up. That would be the last time I would use that telephone.

I hopped in a taxi and went to the restaurant on Via Crescenzio. I inquired as to the availability of a room for a luncheon meeting in two weeks. The manager took me back to the alcove with the curtains.

I pretended to be interested, and sat down in a chair with my back to the wall. I scooted the chair up to the table like I was preparing to eat. Then looked at the manager and started discussing the fee for the room. I said it would be acceptable for the six person meeting I was scheduling, and asked to see the menu and wine list.

The manager quickly stepped out of the room, and went to get the menu and wine list. I ducked down, and placed a small transmitter bug under the table. It would transmit clearly for about 12 hours at a distance of up to 300 feet. I got back in the chair, just before the manager came back in. I looked over the menu and wine list, and said I would like to use the room and have my lunch meeting there. I offered him a deposit equal to about 80 U. S. dollars. He gave me a receipt, and a letter of commitment, and I left. Spending $80.00 to listen to the conversations during the evening would give me a better feel for what was going on.

I walked down the street, found a public phone, and called my contact number again. A meeting was set for 1500. He gave an address and told me to come to the third floor to apartment 3A and ask for Senior Bella.

I hung up, and grabbed a taxi back to my hotel. I took out the colored contact lens, washed the rinse out of my hair, and changed clothes. I combed my hair back in its natural form and put on my glasses.

I went back down and took a taxi close to the meeting address. I found a small café with sidewalk seating, and order a pastry and coffee. I sat down to watch the entry of the building where the meeting would be.

About 30 minutes before the meeting was scheduled, I saw Mr. Martin and two other people go in the front door. I paid by bill and walked over to the building. I walked in and up to the third floor. I found Apartment 3A and knocked on the door. A man opened the door, and I asked for Senior Bella. He looked over his shoulder then stepped back and waved me in.

Mr. Smith was standing in the room. I ignored him and went to a chair with its back to the wall, and said that we seem to have a problem. I discussed in great detail the problems with the information I had been given. He just looked at me and said nothing.

I used the standard negotiation technique of "the first to speak loses" and continued to stare at him. He finally waved his hand and said that he had been assured that the information packet that was given to me was complete in every way.

I immediately listed a number of items that were missing, and that any real observation of the target could not have missed. I told him that if he wanted the job handled, I had to have all the information.

I got up and told him that I would be calling tomorrow morning, to arrange the pickup of the rest of the information. Without another word, I walked out the door and out of the building. It's no fun to play with fire, but I had to get his attention someway.

I grabbed a taxi and went back to the street side café across from the target's normal restaurant. I ordered coffee, and starting waiting for the target to appear. I expected to have a 30 minute wait before my target arrived.

When I saw the target and the body guard coming up the street, I went inside the café and paid my bill, then walked out toward the intersection just west of the café.

I crossed the street and went to the restaurant that the target had entered. Just before I entered, I put what looked like a hearing aid in my right ear. It was really a mini-receiver for the bug I had planted under the table.

I entered the restaurant and went straight to the bar. As I nursed my drink, the first man I had seen last night entered the restaurant. He was immediately escorted to the alcove and the drapes were closed. The conversation was in a foreign language that I did not speak, but was familiar with some of the words. I knew it was Russian. My target said very little, but just seemed to listen. I decided that the real boss of the operation was now giving exact instructions to his bag man.

After about 20 minutes, the first visitor left, and I asked for a table along the wall. I could not see the front door, but had a clear view to the alcove. About thirty minutes later another single man came in and was escorted to the alcove.

Once again the curtain was closed and the conversation began immediately. I recognized the language as Italian, and cursed myself for not bringing a tape recorder. After about 20 minutes, the second visitor left.

I ate my meal and watched people come and go for about 45 minutes, then paid the bill and left. I had my 22 berretta in one coat pocket, and the silencer in the inside pocket.

I walked out and waved down a taxi and went to my hotel. I said good night to the man at the desk, went upstairs, and packed up everything I had. I walked down the back stairs and out of the hotel into the dark alley.

I walked away from the hotel, and waved down a taxi. I asked him to take me to a medium priced hotel, and he took off. Ten minutes later, I got out of the cab, and entered the small hotel. I asked for a room for one night, used a third passport and credit card, and was led to my room. I tipped the bellman, and closed the door. I pushed a large chair against the door, put the berretta with the silencer mounted on the pillow next to me, and went to sleep.

The next morning, I called my contact number from my room, and was given an address and time for my meeting. I changed clothes, repacked the suitcase, and walked out of the hotel. I had two hours until the meeting, so I went back to my original hotel, entered the building from the door on the alley, and went up to my room. I hung up my clothes, put a book by the bed, and left the room. I walked downstairs past the desk man and out to the curb.

I took a taxi to the meeting location, and found a small café with seating by the front window. I had a pastry and coffee, and watched the front door of the building with the meeting address. It was about 45 minutes till the meeting was scheduled, so I expected to see Mr. Smith and company enter the building.

When it was ten minutes past the meeting time, I became concerned as I had not seen Mr. Smith, or any of the other people who had been with him before.

I went to the men's room, and screwed the silencer on the berretta. I then slipped it under my arm with the barrel pointing up and the handle pointing to my front. From that position, I could get to and use the weapon quickly if things went bad. My jacket was not buttoned, so I had ready access to my berretta.

I held my arm close to my side to keep the weapon from slipping, and walked out to the building where the meeting was scheduled to take place. I walked up a flight of stairs to room 2B as I had been told. I knocked on the door, and the same man who opened the door yesterday, was once again the first person I saw. He motioned me into the room, and Mr. Smith was seated on the couch.

When the door was closed behind me, I moved into the room and to the side wall so that I could see the doorman and Mr. Smith without moving my head. I took out the berretta and unscrewed the silencer. Mr. Smith became very pale when he saw the gun.

I asked him if he had the information in a more complete form, and he simply put another folder on the table between us. I picked up the folder, and told him exactly what had transpired to this point. He was upset that I had not trusted him. I told him there was nothing personal involved, just professional attention to detail.

I asked who the first visitor was. He turned out to be a diplomatically covered member of the Soviet Consulate. I thanked him for the information, got up and left the room. I quickly descended the stairs and got out of the building. I jumped into the first taxi that came by and went back to my hotel. Once I was in my room, I sat down to examine the new information.

It was much more complete. It actually had pictures of all of the men I had seen enter the alcove at the restaurant. I had no idea why I was not given this in the beginning, but I was definitely unhappy about it. I finally decided it was typical government intelligence nonsense. Don't tell anyone everything that they should know. As I have said before, if the man doing the work doesn't need to know, who does need to know?

I decided that I would have to take action tonight, as the longer I stayed around, the more likely it was that I would be noticed. It was time to tackle the problem.

I left the hotel and walked down the street to a public phone. I called my shop through a local phone number that I been given. Woody wasn't there yet, but they did some switching, and got him on the phone at his house.

I briefly outlined the irregularities, and asked his opinion. He told me that Mr. Smith was just being childish about anyone questioning him. He said it was a go. I said thanks and hung up.

I immediately went and put on my thin leather gloves, and cleaned the knife, berretta, and silencer so that no prints would be on them.

At 2000 I left the hotel by the door on the alley with my clothes in the suitcase. I tossed the suitcase into a garbage can. I then jumped in a taxi and went to the restaurant where all the business was happening.

I walked back along the route until I found the small alley in the darkened area I had noted yesterday. I waited for them to come by. I had the berretta in my right hand with the silencer mounted, and the knife, with the blade out, in my left hand. I leaned against the wall and held both arms slightly behind me so that if someone happened to see me it would not cause alarm that seeing weapons would cause. After about 30 minutes I heard someone coming. I prepared to move immediately if it was my target, but it wasn't. Another 10 minutes passed by before I heard footsteps again, and this time it was the body guard and the target.

The body guard was about a step ahead of the target. As soon as they had passed me, I stepped out of the shadows and looked back the way they had come. Nobody was in sight, so I turned and followed them.

The body guard must have heard my footsteps because he looked over his shoulder at me. He immediately reached in his coat to get his gun. I raised the berretta and shot him twice. The target was surprised to see his body guard go down then turned to look in my direction. I shot him three times.

I picked up the briefcase, and walked back toward the restaurant where all the meetings had taken place. I did not pass anyone while I was walking, and soon found a storm drain where I dumped the knife, the gun, and the extra clips of ammunition.

I hailed a cab and had him take me to the airport. I found a flight going to Paris, bought a ticket using my original passport and credit card, and walked down toward the gate. I stopped in the restroom before I went through customs, went into a stall, and opened the brief case.

It was half filled with Italian currency. I stuffed the money in a charity donation box located in the airport and pushed the briefcase in a trash bin. At least someone was going to get something positive out of this mission.

Forty-five minutes later I was in the air. The flight to Paris took less than two hours. When I got off, I went to ticketing, and found the next flight to the U.S. I purchased a ticket, and went to the bar. I would have to wait for 7 hours before the flight would leave. When I got back to the U.S.A. and was debriefed by Woody Woodford, I was surprised by his lack of response. He simply said "Thank You", shook my hand, and said go home and relax.

At no time did he show any surprise, or other emotion. I walked out to the car waiting for me, and went home. It took two weeks before I answered the phone, or talked to anybody at the shop or the farm. It was a tough time. I knew that I was just a pawn in a game the government was playing, and if they lost the pawn, well that's just too bad. I had been told that I could quit whenever I wanted to, but I knew better than that. A Shadow Warrior just doesn't just walk away from being **Inside the World of Mirrors**. I realized that my transition was complete.

I was a now a ghost

I didn't exist

I didn't count

They didn't care!

Chapter 12
The Romanian Connection

I was down at the Farm, just keeping sharp on the range one morning, when the range master came out to let me know that visitors were coming out to see me. I got my gear together and headed back to the shop. I had just completed cleaning and storing my LC-1A and scopes when in walked the parade.

Leading the parade was Woody Woodford who was still my primary permanent controller. The last 4 in the line were obviously political hacks. They all wore the same kind of blue pin-striped suit. It was the hallmark of the congressional and white house worker bees.

Woody introduced the worker bees then took them off for a quick tour of the Farm. He came back while they were being led around and asked that I be on my best behavior.

This was a politically driven mission, and the National Security Advisor to the President had sent this team to learn what it would take to get it done.

I was not a happy camper, as every time a politician has gotten involved in something, history had proven that it would end up as a mess and would be page one in all the papers. Woody repeated what he had just said, and I just nodded.

He went off to pick up the political hacks that I would have to deal with. I went down the hall to my locker, cleaned up, and changed into better clothes.

When they came back, Woody walked up in front of the room and began his briefing. Some very special information was coming out of the Soviet Union again. This time it was going to come through Brezoianu 39 in Bucharest, Romania.

That address was the Opera House in Bucharest. In the back of the building, there were several drain pipes running down from the roof. Beside one of the drain pipes was a loose stone. It is actually only a half stone, the rest of the area being used as a dead drop for microfilmed information.

It is one of the most significant dead drops in United States Government's Intelligence history, as it was through this dead drop that information smuggled out of the Chelomei Design Bureau in the Soviet Union came to be available at a critical point in U.S. history. I'm sure you remember the "Cuban Missile Crisis". The information on this microfilm gave the President the knowledge that the missiles in Cuba were not yet functional.

This drop was still being used at the time of this briefing. The American Intelligence community had established a special program just to service this dead drop. It was never approached by anyone associated with the Embassy in Romania. All pick-ups were done by external personnel. Many times they came in as business people trying to sell something to the Romanian government, but most times they came as tourists. They would take several tours that the Romanian government had set up.

One of these tours was an Architectural Tour of the famous buildings in Bucharest. It was one of the most popular tours taken by tourists. The reason this was a perfect cover for servicing the dead drop was that the tour busses stopped and parked behind the Opera House.

At the end of the tour, people would be standing out behind the Opera House waiting to get back on the bus. If you have a crowd around, then a 3 or 4 man team could effectively remove the stone from the wall, pull out the microfilm, and put the stone back in place without being obvious.

This time it would use a 3 man team. They were covered as part of a travel group that went through 3 or 4 countries in about 10 days. Romania was one of these countries because of the legend of Count Dracula. They had an all day tour to the region where the real count had lived. It was the largest tour that the Romanian government ran.

They would tack a second tour, such as the Architectural Tour on to the end of the Count Dracula tour. This was a major source of hard currency for Romania.

This background story gave the visitors a feeling of being on the inside of a very special intelligence mission. My shop had been doing this for many years, as a method of insuring that the politicians in charge of the intelligence budget would not start cutting it down.

This meeting was strictly a political action. In the late 1979, it finally blew up in the shop's face when a political hack leaked the information to make his position look more important.

The political hacks left, and Woody and I went to the real briefing room. Waiting there were two men I had seen around many times, but had never met or worked with. They normally worked the Asian Courier Missions, and had never been in behind the Iron Curtain.

I had been in three times, and it was hard to explain to anyone how difficult it was to do anything because of the size of the Security Services in the Warsaw Bloc countries. East Germany and Bulgaria were by far the most dangerous, but Romania was probably in third place.

We would be going in as an "illegal" (a person with no diplomatic cover) status. The couriers were a little nervous about this, but I was used to it. I seldom had any kind of protection.

I was someone that they could say that they had never known. I was just a ghost of a human being doing nothing more than moving from one picture to the next. I had truly changed over the years to become the ghost that was born on Hill 328 in Cambodia, but only I knew it.

The mission was unusual. It was planned to take place three weeks in the future. This timing was necessary for several reasons. One reason was that it allowed us to be on the tour list for several weeks before going in. This would diminish the security service's attention to us.

Another reason was that the time for the microfilm to work through a set of covert couriers was about two weeks. The information on the microfilm would sit untouched for about a week. The long time between the placement of the microfilm and its retrieval was a major reason that the dead drop had been so successful for so long.

Most security services were able to locate dead drops because they were used often enough to establish a pattern that would cause them to be noticed.

In all the years that it was used, Brezoianu 39 had actually only been serviced 5 times. It was saved for only the most important of deliveries. This would be the 6th time it was used. The 5th time was over two years ago.

The Farm even had a mock-up stone wall with a drain pipe to practice on. It was hidden in the sub-basement of a local warehouse. We would practice the servicing activity under the guidance of the last man to service it.

The next morning we went to the warehouse and down to the sub-basement. The air was stale, and a fine layer of dusk covered the floor. There were no furnishings, only the practice wall and about 15 electrical outlets on other walls. These outlets were used to power extra lighting and cameras. The idea was to learn the action script so well that even the cameras wouldn't see us do it. If the cameras didn't see us, the thinking was that any security service personnel that might be watching would not see us either.

We soon found out how difficult it was to hide our actions from the cameras. It required precise body positioning and movement.

Basically, we were to act like all tourists and take lots of pictures of each other everywhere we went. One of us would take a picture of the other two by a building or whatever we were visiting during the tour. Then the one who took the picture would replace one of the two against the wall, and the one replaced would take another picture.

We would repeat this activity until all three of us had a turn at the camera. The trick was that each picture covered a part of the retrieval process. The first picture would be used to cover the loosening of the stone until it was half out. The second picture would be used to cover the retrieval of the microfilm. The final picture was to push the stone back in till it was flush with the rest of the wall.

Whoever had come up with this dead drop had paid attention to every detail. The stone was the 15th from the bottom in the second row to the right of the drain pipe. It was positioned exactly where someone would put their arm around someone's waist during the taking of a picture.

We came back to practice every other day. We had one chance to get it right on site, so we had to be absolutely perfect in the positioning of our bodies and the hand and arm movements necessary to recover the drop.

We had special signals that the person taking the picture could use if he noticed any possible problem with the security people. Each person in each picture had an exact place and posture to assume. If one of them saw a problem, he would not assume the correct position. The one with the camera would pretend to be having a problem, and we would not continue until he saw that we had resumed the correct positions and postures. This must be what it's like for a magician to do a trick. It's all sleight of hand and misdirection.

We joined the tour group in New York City. We were three brothers, according to our passports. We were from an area that no other member of the tour had come from.

We boarded the plane and flew to England. We cleared customs, and were taken to a hotel to sleep till the next morning. Over the next two days we took a tour of two castles, and the Tower of London, then went to the airport to fly on to the next destination.

Our next stop was Romania. We flew into Bucharest and landed in the late in the evening. I had warned the two couriers of the tiresome customs procedures, and had told them that they would almost always be told that their papers were not correct, or something such as that.

They had to be prepared to react in a very mild and confused way just as anyone who was innocent would act. We had rehearsed them in this process till they felt comfortable handling the customs process.

Just as I had predicted, one of the couriers was given trouble by the customs officials. He handled it well, and was soon outside with his luggage, getting on the bus with the rest of us. They took us from the airport to the Intercontinental Hotel.

This was supposedly the best hotel in the country, but I've seen hotels in Harlem that would put this one to shame. It was definitely something out of the 1950s, with the added oddities that all communist countries seem to find a way to make happen.

The next morning we took the tour to see Count Dracula's castle and a museum that was standing beside it. We came back to the hotel rather late, and went to bed. The next morning we had the Architectural Tour scheduled for 1000.

We ate breakfast early, and walked around the plaza where the hotel was located. We were taking pictures of everything, and each other to help build the cover story as completely as we could.

When we were walking well away from any people or buildings, I reminded them that we were going to do the recovery just as we rehearsed. We went back to the hotel and waited in the lobby with the other tourists. As usual, the bus was late in arriving to pick us up.

The tour guide got us all loaded onto the bus. The tour began by driving to the Government buildings downtown. We were led along while the tour guide talked about the buildings we were seeing.

We continued the picture swap routine in front of every building. In one case we did our picture taking routine twice. Soon we were back on the bus and heading for the next set of buildings. These building were the homes of many of the most influential people in the country.

The tour guide continued to lead us around while pointing out that all of these buildings had been built before 1920. The style was certainly old, but the appearance of the buildings was immaculate. It was obvious that the stone work and bricks had been cleaned and the wood trim looked freshly painted. This was the first area in Romania that looked like something you would find in Germany or France.

We loaded back on the bus and headed for the Opera House. The bus unloaded us behind the building as we had been led to expect. After we were unloaded, the bus drove away. We went around the building to the front and entered the building.

This was obviously the show place of the entire tour. A great deal of time was spent explaining what was special and different about the building. We were then left to wander around inside the building. We were told that the bus would be back in 45 minutes.

They told us to be sure and be back behind the building where we were dropped off by that time. We wandered around the inside for about ten minutes then went outside. We took our series of pictures with the front entry way as our backdrop.

Then we walked around the building to the rear. After about 15 minutes, there were about 25 people standing around waiting for the bus. We prepared to start the retrieval of the microfilm.

I was in the first two pictures. We were almost ready to remove the stone when a local policeman walked up beside us. If there was something we didn't need, it was to be observed by a policeman. I quietly gave the trouble sign to the two couriers. Then I walked out and took a picture of the two couriers standing at the back of the building.

The policeman was standing about 15 feet away from me. There was no way to get the microfilm without his seeing us. My mind was going 100 miles a minute. Then the light bulb went off.

I walked over to the policeman. His English was not the best, but I got him to understand that we wanted a picture of all three of us by the building. I asked if he would be so kind as to take the picture. He shook his head no.

I continued talking to him, and finally got him to take the camera when he saw a ten dollar bill folded under the camera. He finally agreed and I went to stand with the two couriers by the back wall.

I moved them so that when I stood behind them with my arm around the back of the courier next to me I would be able to easily reach the stone. We posed and the policeman put the camera to his eye to take the picture. The courier in the middle put his hand up behind his back and I slipped the stone out and put it in his hand. I reached in and felt the small file container and pulled it out. I slipped it in my pocket, took the stone back and put it back in place.

The entire time involved in this process was about 15 seconds. The guard had snapped a picture, and I walked out to retrieve the camera. I thanked him and noticed that the ten dollar bill had disappeared.

I went back to my two teammates, and we lit of a cigarette and just stood there talking. I noticed that the brick was not pushed all the way back into the wall. I maneuvered a courier to block the policeman's view, and pushed the brick back in with my elbow.

In about 5 minutes the bus pulled up, and we all got on board. My heart was beating very fast. We had pulled it off with a policeman standing 15 feet from us and taking our picture.

When we got back to the hotel, we went up to our rooms. I changed clothes, and while doing so put the microfilm inside a compartment in the heel of my shoe. I finished packing, and went down stairs with my luggage to wait for the bus to the airport.

The bus came, picked us up, and took us to the airport. The customs officers spent a lot of time processing everyone in the tour. I was about halfway back in the line waiting for my turn. When I finally reached the customs desk, I was waved over to the side with my luggage. It was my turn to be harassed just like the courier had been harassed when he came in country.

They had me open my luggage. They removed everything in the bag, and ran their hands over all the inside to see if something was hidden in the lining. Then they had me empty my pockets and put the contents on the table beside my clothes.

The last step in the process made my blood run cold. They told me to take off my shoes. I did as they requested, trying to keep a surprised and confused expression on my face. One of the customs guards took my shoes, turned them upside down, and shook them. When nothing fell out of the inside of my shoes, they set them down on the table with my clothes.

One of the customs guards walked away, while the other one kept pawing through my clothes. Finally he motioned me to pack up the suit case and go down to the gate. The first thing I did was put on my shoes.

I quickly picked up the contents of my pockets, and then repacked the suitcase in record time. I nodded my head to him, and walked away. The plane was sitting on the tarmac. It had a rolling stairway against the planes door, and a small luggage carrier belt running up into the bottom of the plane.

They took my luggage, put it on the carrier, and sent it up inside the plane. I walked up the stairs and went to my assigned seat. It took almost an hour, before everyone was in the plane. We took off shortly after that.

When we arrived in Milan, Italy, the next stop on the tour, my luggage was missing. I made the normal complaints about the missing luggage, and was told that a trace would be made on the luggage.

I left the airport with the clothes on my back. We were conveyed to our hotel by bus again. After checking in, we were told that we should all be back downstairs in two hours. They had dinner reservations for all of us.

I went up the stairs to the third floor where my room was. After 20 minutes, I opened the door and walked down the stairs, through the lobby, and out onto the sidewalk with my camera. I walked about two blocks down the street till I saw a restaurant that I had been told of.

I went past the restaurant, leaned up against the building, and lit a cigarette. Ten minutes later a man walked up to me and asked for a light for his cigarette.

I gave him a book of matches and said to keep them. He asked me if I was an American. I told him that I was Canadian. His reply was Scotch whiskey was the best. This had completed our mutual identity verification.

A car pulled up, and we both got in. We went to a small private airport south of the city. A small propeller driven plane was on the tarmac. We walked to it and got in.

Two hours later I was deposited in the airport in Rome with a diplomatic passport and first class tickets for a flight that left in two hours. I went into a restaurant and had dinner.

Ten hours later I landed in Washington D.C. I breezed through customs and went out on the sidewalk. A limo pulled up and the door opened. Woody was sitting inside. I got in and we took off for the shop.

While we were in transit I took my shoe off, opened the compartment in the heel, and gave Woody the microfilm.

Two hours later I had finished the debriefing, and went out to the waiting limo. It took me home. I never knew what was on the microfilm. I never bothered to ask such a useless question. I was just glad that it was over. Just another trip **Inside the World of Mirrors** where nothing was as real as it seemed to be, and you were lucky if you knew half the truth and were alive at the end.

Chapter 13
Basking with the Basque

I was playing golf when my pager went off. The only reason I looked at the number on the pager was to find out which of two locations I needed to call back. Only one organization had the pager number. This time they wanted me at the shop. That was the good news. I was only a 30 minute drive away.

I finished up my round of golf, loaded my clubs in the car, and headed to the shop. This was not unusual to suddenly change my plans for the day. I knew better than to make any long term appointments because I never knew when a call would come. At least this time it wasn't in the middle of the night.

It was close to 1500 so the traffic was just starting to back up. I pulled off the parkway and drove past the Agricultural Research Station to the large parking lot that sat around the main building.

Since I had no parking permit, I just pulled into the VIP parking area. I got out and walked in the front door. Within 10 minutes Woody Woodford came out and took me to a briefing room.

I was told that the Spanish Government was tired of trying to deal with the Basque Separatist Movement (Euzkade Ta Askatasuna normally referred to as the E.T.A.). The E.T.A. wanted a separate country to be created for them in the northern portion of Spain.

The top people in the organization were living across the border in France. They would slip terrorists across the border, cause some "trouble", and slip them back across the border into France.

The Spanish Government had made a number of overtures to the French Government to get some help in dealing with the E.T.A. While the French had been politically responsive, they never took any action or made any attempt to help the Spanish Government. France didn't want any problems with the Basque in their own country, so they just ignored everything that was happening.

A meeting with a Colonel Garza was scheduled for me in two days. They wanted an intelligence gathering mission to be performed by someone that had no relationship with the Spanish Government. I had been picked, chosen, and otherwise selected to be the errand boy for the U.S. Intelligence community.

Historically, from the days of General Franco to the present, the rank Colonel has been at the sharp point of the sword for everything that happened in the Spanish Government.

It was almost as if the Colonels were a private society within Spanish Government that was charged with actually running the government. The meeting would take place in Madrid.

There would be "Discussions confirming our earlier Understandings". No mention of costs or expenses would be involved. It would be my first meeting with a foreign government that I had done alone. The few times that I had done work for another government, Woody Woodford was always the front man on all contacts.

Woody and I discussed how this meeting should be handled for over 4 hours. Dinner was brought in and we continued to work. When he was finally satisfied that I wouldn't mess up the meeting, he became much more relaxed.

I would work with 4 different sets of passports, documentation, and credit cards. They were preparing them even as we were talking. As usual, I would not have diplomatic immunity. I was just a tourist enjoying Europe.

Late the next afternoon, I would fly out on British Airways to Madrid via Heathrow. My arrival time in Madrid would be about 1200 local time. The meeting was scheduled in at the Cenador de Salvador Restaurant located at Avda de España, 30, Moralzarzal, 28411 Madrid at 2000 that evening.

In spite of what it looks like on the address, the restaurant was about 50 kilometers from Madrid. I would be picked up at my hotel, the Sol Melio Me Madrid Reina Victora, at 1900. It was a five star hotel that catered to old money. I'll say this for the Spanish Government, their hospitality was first rate.

I would not be carrying any of my weapons. The 22 berretta with a silencer and the 22 Winchester with a scope would be delivered by diplomatic courier to the embassy. If I needed them, all I had to do was to call the COS and the embassy.

I went down in the basement at the shop and packed two suitcases. One contained only the finest in apparel from Seville Row in London. The other contained normal tourist and worker type clothing. No matter what I got involved in, I could probably make do with what I was taking.

The next evening I boarded British Airways. I immediately had a couple of drinks, and dozed off to sleep my way across the Atlantic Ocean.

Spanish customs was a quick and painless process. I went out to the taxi line, and waited until I was next in line. I dropped a suit case which popped open because I had opened the latches, and had two people behind me take the next taxi. I pulled my bag back together, got in a taxi, and went to the hotel.

I sat a little sideways in the seat to see if I was being followed. I checked into the hotel under the name that Colonel Garza had been given. I was quickly taken to a 4 room suite, and left to my own devices.

I had converted about $500.00 U.S. Dollars to the local currency at the airport. I kept an additional $3,000.00 U.S. in the safe in my room at the hotel. It was about 1400, so it was time for a leisurely lunch Spanish style.

I went down the restaurant in the hotel and had lunch. I had seen two men in the restaurant when I entered that I had seen sitting in the hotel lobby. Alarm bells went off in my head, but I did not look in their direction again.

My expectations were that Colonel Garza had some watchdogs waiting for me. After lunch I went back up to my room. I cleaned up, got dressed, and waited for my dinner engagement. I didn't leave until the concierge called to say that my car was waiting.

I went downstairs, and the two men I had seen earlier were standing beside a large Mercedes with the door open for me. I said nothing but just got in. No words were exchanged during the entire trip. When we arrived at the restaurant, I was escorted in to a private room. I was introduced to Colonel Garza, and we sat down.

He told me that the fish was excellent, and 2 minutes later we were served. During the meal, the Colonel quietly asked me discretely and indirectly about my background. I told him that I had been of service to my country over 50 times, and was comfortable with the arrangements and accommodations. He smiled, nodded his head, and from then to the end of the meal, we chatted about the tourist activities that I should be sure to make use of. After the 7 course dinner was finally over and cleared, we got down to serious discussions.

They had the last name of a Basque cell leader, Bearaza, and they wanted to know everything I could find out about him and his associates. They could not send Spanish speakers into the area because of the close knit community that the Basque were in.

Any Spanish speaking person would not have a chance of getting any information or doing a successful search. I told him that I would work with only French citizens. They would be mercenaries, and would not care what the job was. The Spanish involvement would never be mentioned outside of the people in this room at the restaurant.

He said that was good, and asked me when I would go to work on his requests. I assured him that within the next 5 to 7 days I would have a staff gathering the information that he wanted. We established a communication link. And we shook hands, and he left.

Five minutes later I was taken downstairs and put in the same car I came in. An hour later I was back at the hotel. It was 0130 local time. I pushed a chair up against the door, and went to sleep.

The next morning, about 1000 I went for a walk and found a public phone. I called the U.S. Embassy and asked for Ernie Williams, COS and the embassy. A minute later he came on the line and I gave him the name that he had been told he would hear from.

He asked me how my flight was. I said my arms are a little tired, but nothing too bad. He said liniment would help. This completed the confirmation of identity. I made arrangements to have the 22 berretta and silencer with 5 clips of ammo to be delivered at the hotel by 1500. He said thank you for the call and hung up.

I walked back to the hotel, and asked when the first flight would be available in the morning to Marseilles in France. He checked and came back with an acceptable schedule. I would fly out at 1100 in the morning, and return by 1400 the day after.

I went up to my room, and waited for the delivery of my weapons. At 1450 a knock on my door brought me to my feet. I went to the door, and the bellman said that the package he was carrying had been left for me at the desk. I took it, tipped him, and closed the door. Inside the box there was the berretta and ammunition I had ordered. I put them all in the room safe with the money I had put away.

I boarded a plane to Marseilles the next morning. I needed to find Giovanni Badeau. He was a mercenary I had worked with before. If he was not gone out on a job, then I would find him at a small bar that catered to ex-Foreign Legionnaires and mercenaries.

Giovanni was the product of a French father and an Italian mother. He looked and dressed like any other working man in the area. I arrived at the bar about 1500 and was told that he was in town, and would probably be in about 2000. I tipped the bartender and said I would be very happy if he happened to come in earlier.

I ordered a drink and went to sit in at the back table in the bar. I never saw the barman call, but about 45 minutes Giovanni walked in and I waved him over. He had two men with him that he sent over to the bar to drink and keep watch.

I ordered drinks for the men at the bar and for Giovanni. In quiet tones, I asked him if he could spare some of his valuable time. He said he was sure he could squeeze me in. With that conversation, I had committed at least $5,000.00 U.S. at a minimum.

I suggested that we all take a walk, and he led the way. We walked about two blocks to a store front. He opened the door with a key, and we went in through the store to the back room. He left one of the men in the store area to keep watch.

I pulled out the information and pictures that I had on Agoztar Bearaza. We discussed how many men it would take to do the surveillance. He thought three more men with him would do a good job. He said they would go to Biarritz, France the next day and start working.

I gave him my room number at the hotel in Madrid, and told him to call me as soon as he started making progress. He took me to a small hotel near the airport, and made arrangements for me to be taken to the airport the next morning. It all went as planned and I caught my flight back to Madrid.

I stopped in the Madrid airport and used a public phone to call a number I had in Madrid. The number automatically connected me with the shop's operational control room. I gave them a quick brief to give to Woody, hung up, and went out of the air port to my hotel. I was just a little late for lunch, and way too early for supper by Spanish standards, so I went to a little bar down the street and had a couple of drinks.

I went to a couple of night clubs where Colonel Garza had suggested I go to enjoy the show. His suggestions were excellent, and while I was enjoying myself, I called it a night at 2330 and went back to my hotel and to bed.

Giovanni would call me as soon as he got started. Until then, I was just a tourist. Two long and tedious days later Giovanni called and gave me an address to come to in Biarritz.

I checked out of the hotel, went to the airport, rented a car, and drove to Biarritz. It was a common destination on the coast, and a popular with vacationers. I got a local map, and drove around until I found the house address I had been given.

I parked the car across the street from the house. I put my 22 berretta and silencer in one pocket and 3 clips of ammo in another. When I was walking up to the door Giovanni opened it before I even knocked on the door. I walked inside and he handed me a glass of cognac with a grin. He said that this was going to be easy money for him, and expensive information for me.

This was no surprise. I knew what I was getting into when I went to see him. He had found our target, and surprised me by telling me that he had slept at one address each night, and went to another address first thing every morning. Both were visits to lovers he was playing with, but one at night was his girl friend and the one in the morning was his boy friend. Giovanni commented that he was certainly a man of much vigor and had an open minded disposition. I just grinned and lit up a cigarette to go with the Cognac.

He had both of the addresses, the make and model of his car, and the license plate number for me now. He also had the name of the girl, and would have the man's name in a couple of hours.

He had also seen him in a coffee shop with two young men. When they left the coffee shop, the two men went in one direction and our target went in another. He put one of his crew on following the two men. He personally kept watch on Bearaza

After about an hour, a wrinkled little old man came in the door. This man had the address where the two people from the coffee shop had gone. He also had the name of the boy friend and his telephone number.

Over the course of the next 2 days his team found three more potential terrorists, and knew where they lived as well. We now had a fairly firm fix on Bearaza activities. I used the phone and called Colonel Garza. I gave him the information, and requested further instructions. He was surprised by how fast it had happened.

It was quick because the stupid Basque terrorists were actually listed in the phone book. I had heard of stupid, but being a terrorist with a known address and phone number marked them as far beyond stupid. I didn't tell Colonel Garza that, but I did find it amusing. Garza said he would get back to me tomorrow.

I hung up and we put the rest of Giovanni's team out watching the other terrorists. Now it was time for dinner. In France, dinner was anytime after 1800 and before 0100. They just wanted you to come in and spend money. After dinner we went back to the house that Giovanni had rented. I went to bed and he sat up waiting for his team to return.

The next morning, I was on my way to breakfast with Giovanni when he saw a newspaper with a front page story about an attempted murder of a top level individual in Spanish Intelligence.

The attempt was quickly connected to the Basque because the only person who survived the attempt was a member of the E.T.A. We grabbed some pastries, and hurried back to the apartment. When we got there I had a number to call back. Colonel Garza had called for me.

I called Colonel Garza and listened to the story of the assassination attempt on a man that I got the impression was his boss. It could have actually worked, but the Basque had started shooting at the first car to come out of the government compound, and the supposed target was in the second car. Only one person survived from the first car. The official's car escaped unscathed. The Basque were killed by the local security team that was in the 3rd car with additional support personnel that came out of the compound.

The high ranking Spanish official was screaming for action to be taken. I told Colonel Garza that I would call him back in a couple of hours. Then I called the number in Madrid and was connected to the shop's operations control room. I gave them my number, and said I had to talk to Woody immediately. I didn't care that it was very early in the morning. Just make the call and have him call me.

I hung up and looked at Giovanni. I told him that he might get to make some more money. He just shook his head and grinned. Twenty minutes later the phone range and Woody was on the line. It was not a secure line, so we had to talk around the problem but were still able to communicate clearly.

I finally told Woody that we were probably going to be asked to be a substitute batter in the 9th inning. He thought it over for a moment, and told me as long as I was comfortable with the pitch count, he felt comfortable in letting me take the swing. I hung up and immediately called Colonel Garza.

I had to hold for about 3 minutes until he came to the phone. He admitted that he had been in direct communication with some very important people. Those people felt corrective action must take place immediately. He said he thought 3 to 1 were good odds. I said it would seem to be likely, and that I would get back to him.

I turned to Giovanni and said the price just went up. I told him to go get some plastic explosive, and couple of igniters, and some hard weapons. He said it cost about $2,000.00 U.S. I handed him the money and he went off to get everything I told him. Three hours later he was back with his crew and two cars with their trunks full.

We talked back and forth till we decided how we could do the job properly. Then I called Colonel Garza and told him that it appeared that the shipment had been damaged, and asked for him to authorize me to negotiate an appropriate settlement. He said, " Hold on " and went away for about 3 minutes. He came back and said that he would recognize my authority to complete the necessary negotiation in whatever way I felt was correct. He did emphasize that this was causing him a great deal of trouble, and that he expected the settlement to be very healthy. I said, "Yes sir, Thank you sir," and hung up.

I told Giovanni that his commission just went up. He grinned and said when does it happen? I told him tonight. He sent one of his runners out to bring in the rest of his team. I had him put one of his crew on the Bearaza house to watch where he parked his car.

At 2300 hours we got in one of the cars and drove near to where Bearaza lived. We put a lookout about 100 meters away down the street in both directions. Each sentry had a small portable radio to tell us if any traffic was approaching.

Giovanni and I walked down the street and stopped in a dark place about 10 meters from the target's car. We got down and crawled through the shadows and got under the car. I wrapped about 2 pounds of plastic explosive around the gas tank, inserted an igniter, and tied a string from the igniter to the nearest back wheel. I left slack in the string so that the car would have to move about 25 feet forward for the string to wrap around the axle and trip the igniter. We then crawled back to the dark area. We stood up and brushed our clothes off, and continued our stroll down the street.

It was now 0400, and Bearaza would be coming out around 0800 to leave as usual. We walked down the street about 200 meters to the rear of the car, found a dark place to sit down, and waited for the show. At the same time, two other members of Giovanni crew were waiting outside the other terrorist's residence to introduce them to Mr. Uzi from Israel.

At 0815 Bearaza walked out and got in the car. He waved to the girl standing in the door and drove off. He barely got out of his parking spot when the explosion occurred. We got in our car and drove back to the rented house.

About 40 minutes later his crew that had been watching the other house came walking in. They had no weapons, but talked in French to Giovanni. He told me they had hidden the weapons, and the two targets were pretending to be Swiss cheese now.

I called Colonel Garza and told him that the negotiations were complete, and that we had received excellent value for the shipment's damage. He thanked me and asked me to be sure to come and see him if I ever came back to Madrid. I hung up the line.

I pulled Giovanni aside and asked if an additional $10,000.00 U.S. was OK? He shook my hand and told his boys to go home. I called back to the shop through the Madrid number, and gave them the information to get Giovanni and his team paid.

I told them I would clean up some details, and be back in a couple of days. Since I was already at a coastal resort, I might as well take a couple of days to enjoy it.

It had been just one more trip into
"It Never Happened Land"

<u>Inside the World of Mirrors</u>

<u>Epilogue</u>

The story of **<u>Inside the World of Mirrors</u>** does not stop here. Remember that these missions were only a very small part of 83 different operations. This book was written to explain and honor the personnel that worked Special Intelligence Operations. Everything was done off the books with no written records that I ever saw.

My career ended when I was seriously injured during an operation in Germany. After a long period in the hospital, including time at Walter Reed Medical Center, I was retired for medical reasons.

From the first day of my retirement I was plagued by nightmares and flashbacks. Nobody in the medical profession had ever heard of Post Traumatic Stress Disorder. It was a condition that beat me down for many years. I still spend many nights reliving what went wrong. I owe a debt to those who worked with me, but didn't come back, to at least tell part of the story.

It is my hope that this book will possibly help other veterans face their issues. The cost of every war ever fought continued to be paid for long after it was officially over. Many of the veterans who participated in these conflicts continue to pay the price for as long as they live.

About the Author

J. Max Taylor was born in Oklahoma City, Oklahoma in Feb 1948. He was an only child and led a normal life through high school. He received his draft notice in late 1967. When he reported to the draft processing center he went through all the normal physical and intellectual testing that every draftee went through. At the end of all the testing, he was taken aside and offered a special position in military intelligence. If he accepted, he would have a three year commitment to the U.S. Army. He accepted the offer, and in doing so he changed the course of his life. He was trained in special intelligence operations activities, attached to special duty with another organization, and was sent to Korea as an intelligence editor. From this point forward, till 1976, his book, Inside the World of Mirrors tells the compelling story of a world that very few people knew existed. He was medically retired in late 1976.

From that time on he has lived in a world of recurring nightmares. The memories of the bad things that happened were never forgotten. He returns every night to the horror and terror that he had experienced. At that time there was no name for his condition. Now it is known as Post Traumatic Stress Disorder (PTSD). He still is under care by the Veterans Administration for these problems to this day.

He went on with his life to become a successful businessman doing business all around the world. In 2000 an accident aggravated the PTSD. Part of the Veterans Administration Program he was in was Psychological Counseling. He was told to write down his experiences, and read them over and over to help deaden the pain and suffering. "Inside the World of Mirrors" is a result of this process.

Today he lives in Phoenix, Arizona with his wonderful supportive wife Dorothy.

CPSIA information can be obtained at www.ICGtesting.com
Printed in the USA
BVOW08s1651270913

332323BV00003B/3/P